W9-BRM-840

14.95

GEOGRAPHY
for FUN
PROJECTS

Children's Department
Marlborough Public Library
35 W. Main St.
01752

Pam Robson

Copper Beech Books
Brookfield, Connecticut

© Aladdin Books Ltd 2001

Produced by
Aladdin Books Ltd
28 Percy Street
London W1P OLD

First published in the United States
in 2001 by
Copper Beech Books,
an imprint of
The Millbrook Press
2 Old New Milford Road
Brookfield, Connecticut 06804

ISBN 0–7613–2279–5

Editor: Kathy Gemmell

Designer: Simon Morse

Illustrator: Tony Kenyon

Picture researcher: Brian Hunter Smart

Printed in UAE

All rights reserved

Cataloging-in-Publication Data is on
file at the Library of Congress.

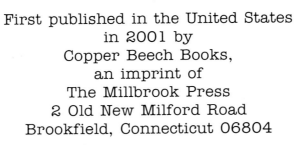

The author, Pam Robson, is an experienced teacher.
She has written and advised on many books for children
on geography and science subjects.

CONTENTS

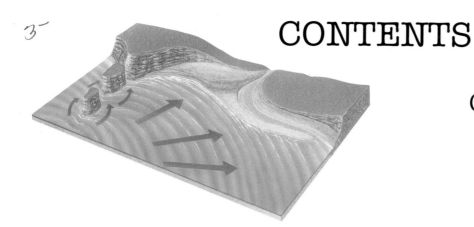

3

INTRODUCTION

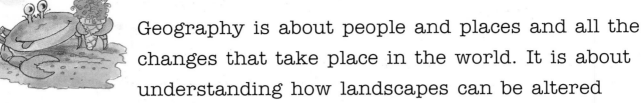

Geography is about people and places and all the changes that take place in the world. It is about understanding how landscapes can be altered over time by natural processes like floods and earthquakes, or by human activity. Geography is about recording these changes. It is about discovering how animals live in harmony with their surroundings, both on the land and at sea, and about studying the effects that pollution can have on an ecosystem. Geography is about the many different ways in which people use the world's resources.

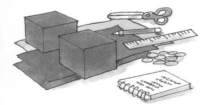

1 Look for numbers like this. Each step for the projects inside the book has been numbered this way. To draw the maps and make the models shown in each project, make sure that you follow the steps in the right order.

FEATURE BOXES
● Look for the feature boxes on each double page. They either give further information about the project on the page, or they suggest other interesting activities for you to do.

WHAT'S HAPPENING

- The What's Happening paragraphs explain the geography behind the projects you do or make.
- The Helpful Hints on some pages give you tips for doing the projects.
- Look at the Glossary at the back of this book to find out what important words mean.
- Always use the most up-to-date maps, atlases, websites, and reference books.
- Use the atlas index to find the location of any place you are looking for.

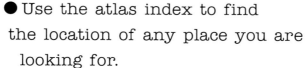

WARNING
- This sign means that you must be careful. Ask an adult to help you when you need to use a sharp tool, a hot liquid, or an electrical appliance. When collecting information for projects, always let an adult know where you are going and what you are doing.

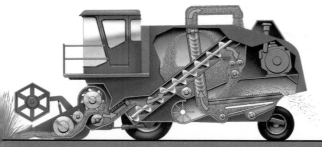

CHAPTER 1

Maps and Plans

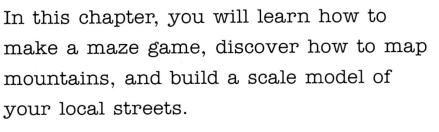

There are many different ways to find your way from place to place. You can follow signposts on the streets to get to wherever you want to go.

If there are no signposts, you can look at landmarks, such as a hill or a particular building. Many people use maps and plans to find their way around.

In this chapter, you will learn how to make a maze game, discover how to map mountains, and build a scale model of your local streets.

CONTENTS

LEFT AND RIGHT

Drivers on a trip read road maps or follow signposts to find out when to turn left or right. Hikers use compasses and maps to find their way. All travelers look for landmarks, such as a particular tree, hill, or building, to help them recognize where they are. Inside mazes there are many turnings, but no landmarks or signposts to point the way.

AMAZING MAZE

Make this maze game and help the elephant and giraffe take all the correct turns to reach the water hole.

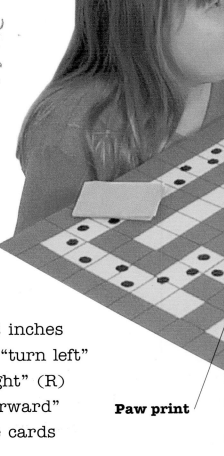

Paw print

1 Copy the African grassland maze in the photograph on a squared board. Draw the pathways first, then decorate them with paw prints.

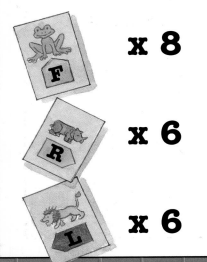

x 8

x 6

x 6

2 Cut out twenty pieces of stiff cardboard measuring 2 inches by 3 inches. Design six "turn left" (L) cards, six "turn right" (R) cards, and eight "go forward" (F) cards. Decorate the cards with different animals.

3 Make an animal counter for each player by drawing a picture on a circle of stiff cardboard and gluing it on a bottle top. If you have toy animals, you could use them instead. Place the counters at the entrance to the maze.

4 The aim of the game is to reach the water hole first. Stack the cards face down. Take turns picking a card. Turn your counter in the direction of the arrow on the card. If you pick a "go forward" card, you can move to the next junction, but only if you are facing the right way. If you can't move, miss your turn. Replace the cards at the bottom of the pile.

MORE IDEAS

● Play again—in reverse. This time, begin at the water hole. The first one to reach the entrance to the maze is the winner.

● Practice giving directions. Ask a friend to find the way from your school to your home, or from one classroom to another. Write down when to turn left or right and whether there are any landmarks to watch for.

NORTH OR SOUTH?

A long time ago, ships had to sail in sight of land to know where they were. Sailors found their way using landmarks. Then it was discovered that magnetic stones called lodestones pointed toward north when suspended. These were the first compasses. Sailors were then able to sail away from coasts to discover new lands. The first maps had compass faces pointing toward the Orient (the east), which was believed to be the center of the world.

COMPASS FACE

Finding the way with a compass and map is now called orienteering. To do any orienteering, you need to know the points on the compass. Make a compass face to help you remember them.

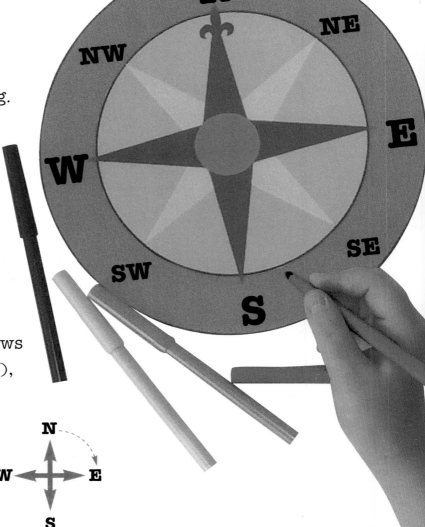

1 Use a ruler to draw a four-point compass face. This shows the four main directions: north (N), east (E), south (S), and west (W). Label them clockwise from the top. Use a protractor to draw more accurately: the clockwise turn between each point is a right angle of 90 degrees.

2 To make an eight-point compass face, draw lines halfway between each of the four main points. Mark these directions NE, SE, SW, NW. Color your compass face. On early maps, north was shown by a fleur-de-lis design like the one shown here. The clockwise turn between each of the eight points is half of a right angle, which is 45 degrees.

HELPFUL HINTS

● Think of a saying to help you remember the clockwise order of north, east, south, and west, such as "Nine, Eight, Seven, Wait."

● Find north by pointing the hour hand of a watch toward the Sun. (Make sure the watch is telling the right time!) Lay the head of a matchstick halfway between the hour hand and twelve, as shown below. The match head will now be pointing south and the other end will be pointing north.

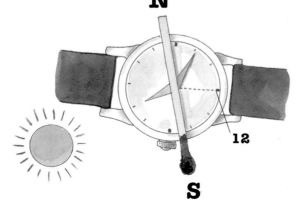

TAKING BEARINGS

● You can figure out the exact position of a landmark by measuring where it is in relation to a fixed position. This is called taking a bearing. Bearings are worked out by measuring angles clockwise from north.

● Choose a landmark that you can see from your yard or school, and work out its bearing. First find north. You can do this using a watch (see left) or by lining up north on a map with north on an orienteering compass. Now measure the clockwise turn from north to the direction of the landmark. This is its bearing.

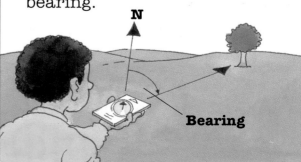

Bearing

BIRD'S-EYE VIEW

Objects look different when they are viewed from above. A bird in the sky sees everything below in 2D (two dimensions) because objects on the ground look flat. Birds cannot see how high objects are. Someone standing on the ground sees the same objects in 3D (three dimensions). They *can* see how high the objects are. A plan of an object or place is always drawn in 2D. A plan is a bird's-eye view.

3D TO 2D

To make a yellow bus drive along this 2-D street plan, you will need two button magnets, a length of dowel, a large sheet of white cardboard, a small sheet of thin yellow cardboard, colored paper, scissors, and glue.

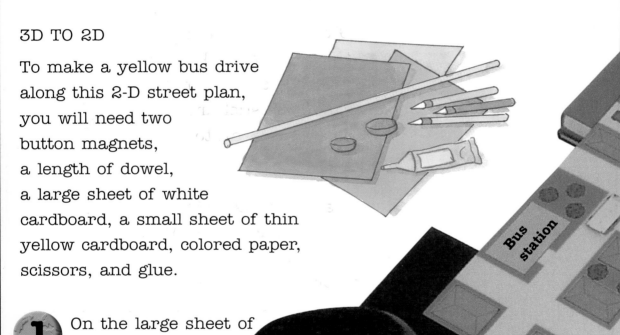

1 On the large sheet of cardboard, draw some streets, or cut them out from paper and paste them on. You can make them up or copy the streets in the photograph. Make sure you leave spaces to put in buildings.

2 The 2-D shapes, or symbols, drawn in the left column of the key below show what objects look like from above. Each 2-D shape represents a 3-D object, like a house, a car, or a tree. Draw and color the 2-D shapes onto your plan.

 = **House**

 = **Car**

 = **Apartment building**

= **Tree**

3 Support the plan on some thick books to leave a space beneath. Now draw and cut out a 2-D bus from yellow cardboard. Make sure it is the right size to fit your street plan. Glue a button magnet to the bottom of the bus.

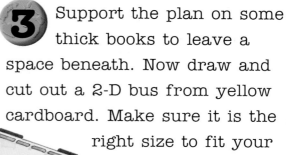

4 Glue another magnet to the dowel to make a stick magnet. Place the bus on the plan. Move the stick magnet underneath the plan to make the bus go.

5 Now write a story describing how the bus gets from one place to another on your plan. Put in landmarks and say where the bus turns.

School

The bus drives out of the bus station and turns left. It drives past the trees on the left and turns right onto Meadow Road. At the apartment building, it turns left onto Main Street, then right onto School Lane. It stops outside the school.

MORE IDEAS
● Make sure your street plan has a compass face marked on it. Now write directions for the route of the yellow bus using N, E, S, and W instead of left and right.

BIGGER AND SMALLER

Bees are much smaller than elephants. But a picture of a bee can be larger than the bee really is, while a picture of an elephant can be smaller than a real elephant. In the same way, a plan or map of a place is much smaller than the real place. Drawing something smaller or bigger than it really is, but keeping it exactly the same shape, is called drawing to scale.

1 Choose a large picture of a famous landmark from a magazine. Glue the picture onto a sheet of paper and draw a grid of large squares over it.

SHRINK THAT PICTURE

To draw a picture to scale, you need graph paper. To reduce the size, use paper with smaller squares, but keep the number of squares the same.

2 On graph paper with small squares, count and cut out the same number of squares that you drew on the large grid. Glue your small grid onto cardboard. Now copy the shape of the picture carefully, square by square, onto the smaller grid.

The famous landmark in this picture is the Taj Mahal in India.

PLAYGROUND PLAN

Draw a scale plan of a playground or park close to where you live. You can measure distances by taking paces (steps), so you don't need a tape measure. Tell an adult what you are planning.

● You will need a pencil and some paper.

First find out which way is north (see page 11). Then pace off the size of the area. Write down how many paces you take in each direction. Note where the entrances and exits are. Sketch the position of objects, such as trash cans and benches.

● Use half-inch graph paper to draw out your plan. One pace on the ground can stand for $1/2$ inch on your plan. This means that your scale is $1/2$ inch = 1 pace. Write this on your plan. Draw a compass face. Use 2-D symbols to show the position of objects in the playground.

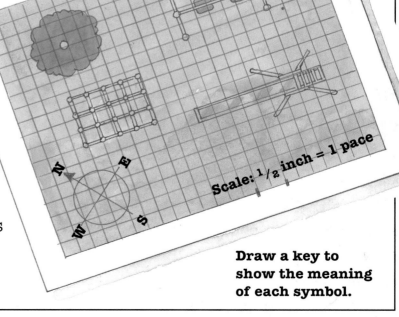

Playground

Scale: $1/2$ inch = 1 pace

Draw a key to show the meaning of each symbol.

PLANS AND SYMBOLS

A plan or map needs to be large-scale in order to show important details like paths and houses. Large-scale means that the map shows lots of detail but only a small area. Most countries have large-scale maps showing different parts of the country. The United States Geological Survey (USGS) makes such maps. Street plans are even larger scale than USGS maps—they even show the names of roads and buildings. Buildings often act as landmarks.

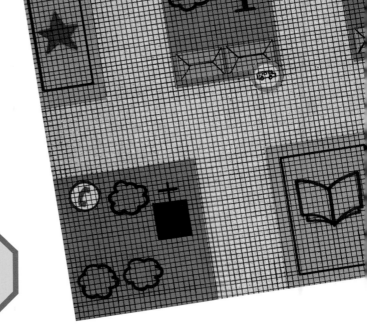

LARGE-SCALE STREET PLAN

Make a large-scale street plan to show the position of the different buildings on a street near your house or school.

1 Ask permission from an adult to carry out a street survey. Always work with a friend, and watch for traffic. Pace off distances between buildings and write down the measurements. Note down the position of each building and what it is used for. Find north (see page 11).

2 Use the measurements to draw a street plan onto half-inch graph paper. Use a scale of $1/2$ inch equals one pace. Draw a compass face.

3 Design 2-D symbols for the different buildings and draw them on your plan. Draw a key for the symbols.

KEY TO PLAN

Keys explain the meaning of colors and symbols used on maps and plans. The key below explains the symbols used on the street plan.

 Police station

 Church

 Library

 Post office

 Private house

 Bus stop

 Bridge

 Theater or Movie house

 Public telephone

 Railroad

 Coniferous tree

 Broad-leaved tree

HELPFUL HINTS

● Some symbols are international and are understood worldwide. Look at the key box above or the key on a USGS map of a town or city for ideas for symbols, or you can make up your own.

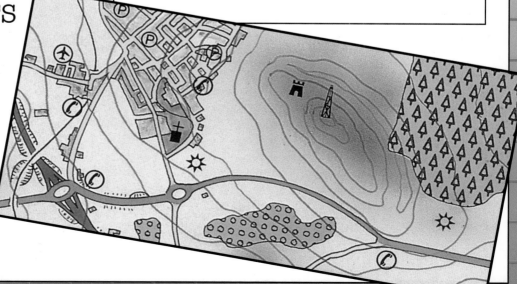

READING STREET PLANS

Street plans show the 2-D shapes and positions of different buildings and objects, but they cannot show the height of buildings. There are many different kinds of homes. Some people live in apartments, which can be in tall buildings. Others live in houses. A 3-D model of a street can show the height of all the buildings.

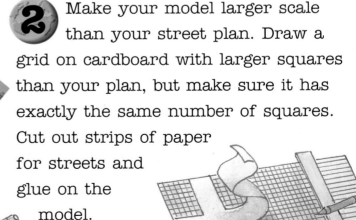

HIGH HOPES

From your street plan, you can construct a 3-D model of a real place. Use paper, cardboard, and clean junk materials or natural materials like twigs and pebbles.

1 First, you need more information about the buildings on your street plan. Take photographs or make drawings of them. Count the number of floors in each building.

2 Make your model larger scale than your street plan. Draw a grid on cardboard with larger squares than your plan, but make sure it has exactly the same number of squares. Cut out strips of paper for streets and glue on the model.

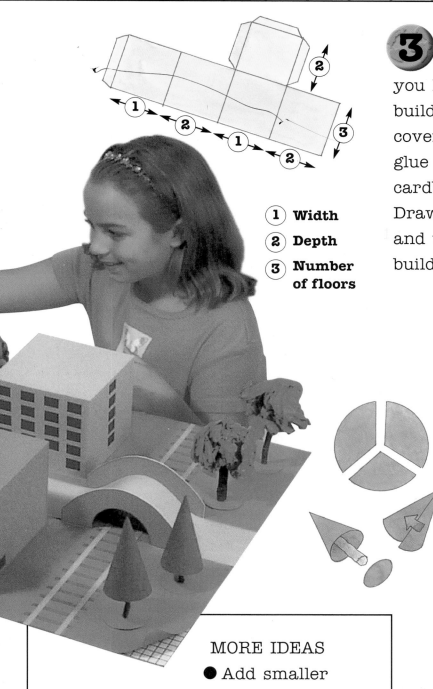

3 Draw a 2-D pattern on cardboard for each building. Make sure you know how wide and deep each building is (count the squares it covers on the plan). Score, fold, and glue the pattern. Fold more cardboard for a roof. Draw or glue on doors and windows. Place the buildings on the model.

1 **Width**
2 **Depth**
3 **Number of floors**

4 Shape some pine trees from cones of green paper, as shown. Make broad-leaved trees from crumpled tissue paper. Make tree trunks from twigs. Glue the trunks onto cardboard bases or push them into clay. Position your trees on the model.

MORE IDEAS
● Add smaller objects to your model, like trash cans and telephone booths. Make signposts and traffic lights.
● Does the road have a pedestrian crossing? Make cars and trucks from clay.

HELPFUL HINTS
● Make features like bridges from colored paper and cardboard.
● Finish buildings by painting them. Do any painting before placing the buildings on the model.
● Make sure any entrances face the right way.

COLORS AND CONTOURS

Small-scale maps cover a wider area than large-scale ones, but do not show as much detail. The shape of large areas of land can be shown on small-scale relief maps. Different colors are often used to show the height of the land. On large-scale maps, the height of the land may be shown by lines called contours. Contours are lines joining places that are the same height above sea level.

SINK A MOUNTAIN

Contour lines show the height of the land in 2D. Make a 2-D contour map by taking measurements from a sinking clay mountain.

1 You will need some clay, a straight-sided plastic bowl, a pitcher of water, a ruler, and a coffee stirrer.

2 Shape a mountain from clay and put it inside the bowl. Place a ruler upright against the side of the bowl.

3 Pour in one inch of water. Use the coffee stirrer to mark a line around the mountain at the water level. Pour in another inch and mark a line at the new water level. Repeat until the water reaches the summit (top) of the mountain.

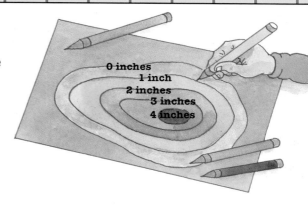

0 inches
1 inch
2 inches
3 inches
4 inches

4 Lift the mountain out of the bowl. Look at it from above and observe the pattern of the lines. Draw a contour map, like the one above, of what you see. Write the correct measurements on the contour lines. Color the spaces between the contours in different shades.

RELIEF MAPS

● Look for small-scale relief maps in an atlas. Some relief maps look like 3-D pictures. Hill shading is used so that hills and mountains—like the Dolomites, Apennines, and Alps shown on this map of Italy—look like real hills and mountains. Different colors often show height above sea level. Sometimes crosshatching is used to show the shape of high ground.

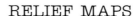

Dolomites

Alps

Po Valley

Apennines

ITALY

SICILY

FIXING POSITION

Describing the position of an object on a page, when there are many objects scattered at random, is tricky. A grid laid over the page makes it much easier. The exact position of every object can then be given using a grid reference, which is the column name followed by the row number.

BIRTHDAY PUZZLE

Send a coded birthday message using a grid. To decode the message, you have to decode the grid references listed in the correct order.

1 Fold a sheet of cardboard in half. Cut a grid of 8 x 11 squares from 1-inch graph paper. Glue it to the front of the cardboard. Cut the board to size if necessary. Leave spaces to write in column names and row numbers.

Leave space for column names along the bottom.

Leave space for row numbers up the left-hand side.

2 Now write each of the letters of the alphabet in a square on the grid. Jumble the letters so you do not read them in order. Draw party objects in the empty squares.

3 From left to right along the bottom of the grid, fill in the column names A to G. Up the left-hand side of the grid, fill in the row numbers 1 to 10. Leave the bottom left square blank.

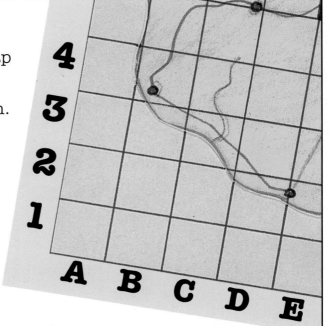

4 Inside the card, write grid references for each of the letters of the message you want to write. Make sure you write them in the correct order. Use the grid to work out the message below.

A5	B9	A10	A10	B6
E10	F8	C8	F6	A5	A7	B9	B6
B9	D3	B4	E1	

GRID MAPS

● In an atlas, a grid map with numbered spaces can cover a whole region. Each square has a grid reference. This makes it easy to locate a particular place on the map, such as a town or city. On this map, there is a town in square B4.

FINDING THE WAY

A routefinder map is larger scale than a country map. It covers a smaller area, and is divided into squares by a numbered grid. Hikers use routefinder maps because they show paths and landmarks. Routefinder maps are different in different countries.

FINDING THE WAY

On this routefinder map, a grid reference with four figures in it refers to the southwest (SW) corner of a particular square on the map. Can you find the church on this routefinder?

1 The four-figure grid reference for the church is 03, 06. Count along the bottom to 03, then count up to 06, and you are at the SW corner of the square with the church in it.

2 There are two bridges marked on the map. Can you find them? One bridge is in square 02, 05. The other bridge is in square 07, 08. Remember to count along the bottom first, and then up to the correct square.

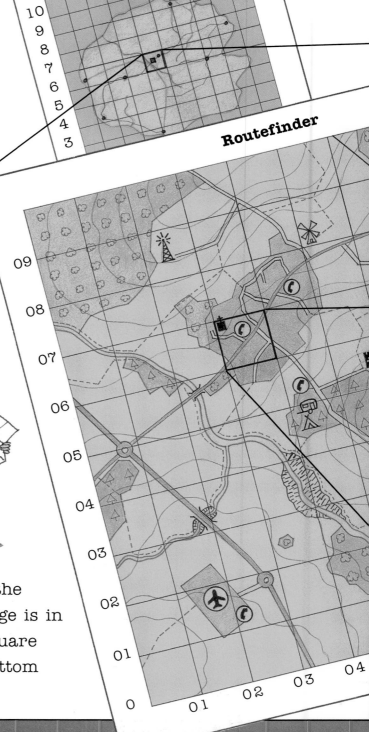

Country map

Routefinder

3 Imagine a magnifying glass placed over square 03, 06. Now imagine that square divided up again by a grid of 100 smaller squares. This lets you see much more detail on that section of the map. It is now a street plan. You can now give a six-figure grid reference, which describes the exact position of a landmark inside the 100 squares on the grid.

MORE IDEAS

● Can you think what kind of map a cyclist needs? Like a hiker, who needs to know where the best footpaths are, a cyclist needs to locate good bicycle routes.

● Look at the street plan. Which feature is next to the police station, at grid reference 034, 066?

Street plan

4 On the street plan, the reference for the church is 031, 069. Can you find the police station? (Look on page 17 if you can't remember the symbol.) Its grid reference is 035, 066.

PICTURE MAPS

Maps are designed differently to highlight particular features of a place. Relief maps show the shape of the land. Political maps show countries, their capital cities, and their borders. Thematic maps tell us interesting facts about different regions. They give information about weather and climate, farming, and wildlife. Maps like this need a key. Picture maps can tell a story without a key because pictures are used instead of symbols.

PICTURE THIS

Make a picture map of your favorite place. It may be a town, a city, or a country that you have visited on vacation.

1 If you have chosen a country, copy its shape from an atlas. For a city, draw a map of the region. Draw and color pictures of the things you like about the place you have chosen. You can also stick on photographs or pictures from magazines.

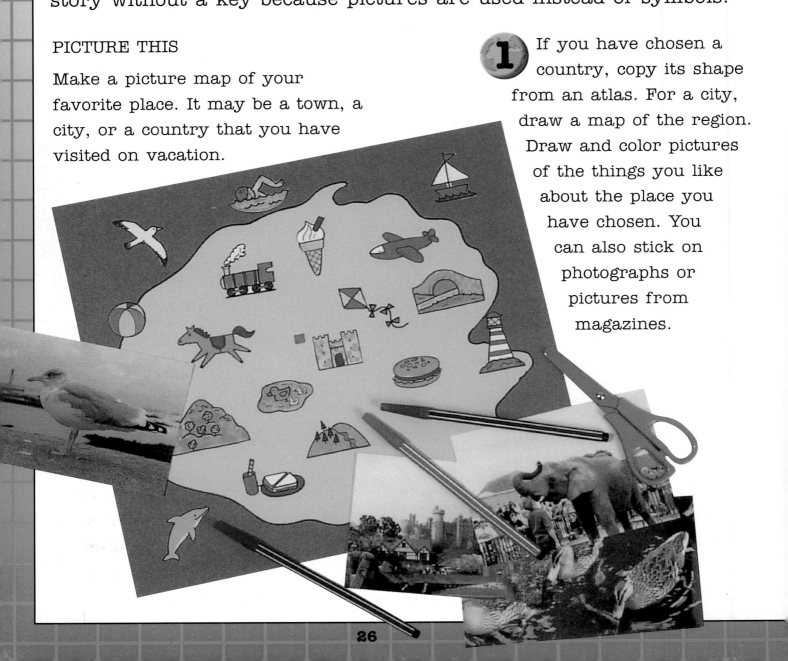

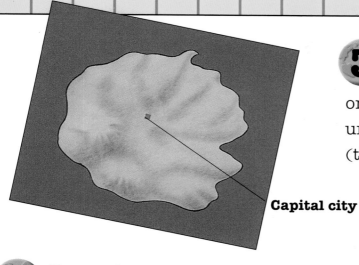

Capital city

3 Political maps of districts use colors to show different counties or regions. Is your favorite place in an urban area (a town) or a rural area (the countryside)?

2 Try to find a relief map of your favorite place in an atlas. Do you remember whether it is flat or mountainous? A relief map like this one shows the shape of the land as a 3-D picture. Other relief maps have contours showing height above sea level.

WEATHER MAPS

● Weather maps use symbols that can be understood anywhere in the world because they are like pictures.

● Look at weather maps on TV. What kind of weather did you have on vacation? Was it sunny or rainy?

● Make weather pictures for your vacation map. What kind of climate does your vacation place usually have?

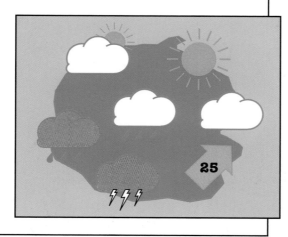

25

4 One kind of thematic picture map is a farming map, which shows where food is grown. Foods that come from your favorite place might be sold in supermarkets on the other side of the world.

COUNTRIES AND CONTINENTS

The world is divided into seven large landmasses called continents. Each country of the world is part of a continent. The United States is a country on the continent of North America. Egypt is a country on the continent of Africa. France is a country on the continent of Europe.

COUNTRY MAP

To make this collage map of the country of Italy, you will need an atlas, a piece of cardboard, colored paper, glue, scissors, colored pencils, clay, and some coffee stirrers.

1 Find Italy in an atlas. Look closely at its shape. Do you think it looks like a boot? Copy or trace the shape of Italy onto the piece of cardboard. Color it in, then use clay to stick coffee stirrers around the edge for your coastline. Break the stirrers to get the right shape.

2 Copy Italy's flag and glue it onto your map. Show the position of Rome, the capital city. Now glue on pictures of things you know about Italy. Look at other kinds of maps to help you. You can even glue on some dried pasta!

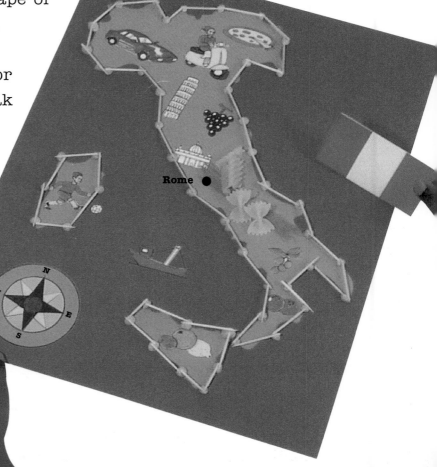

Rome ●

CONTINENT PUZZLE

The seven continents are North America, South America, Oceania, Africa, Asia, Europe, and Antarctica. On this page are the outlines of six of them, each in a different color. They are not in their correct positions. Can you find the shape of each one and arrange them correctly?

On many world maps, including the projection shown below, Antarctica is not shown.

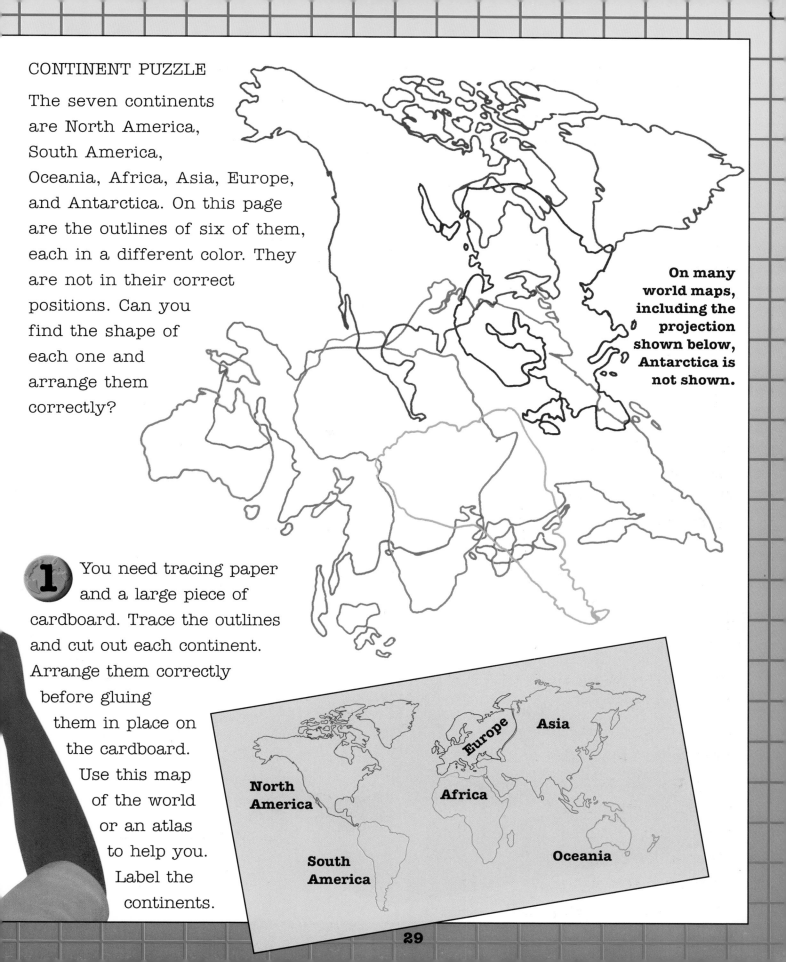

1 You need tracing paper and a large piece of cardboard. Trace the outlines and cut out each continent. Arrange them correctly before gluing them in place on the cardboard. Use this map of the world or an atlas to help you. Label the continents.

North America

South America

Europe

Asia

Africa

Oceania

CHAPTER 2

Mountains and Our Moving Earth

The shape of the land is being changed all the time by volcanic eruptions, slow-moving glaciers, and earthquakes. The hot, liquid rock deep inside the Earth causes tectonic plates to move and, eventually, collide.

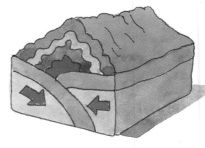

When they collide, rocks are forced upward, and mountains are formed. Ice, wind, and rivers all cause rock to erode, or wear away, which slowly changes the shape of mountains. In this chapter, you will make a continents jigsaw puzzle, construct a rift valley model, and even build your own glacier.

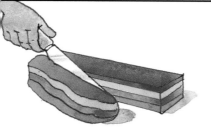

CONTENTS

INSIDE THE EARTH

At the center of Earth is a hard inner core of metallic rock. It is surrounded by an outer core of hot, liquid rock, called magma. Next is a thick layer called the mantle, made up mainly of hard rock with some parts of magma. The magma causes rock in Earth's thin top layer, called the crust, to move around.

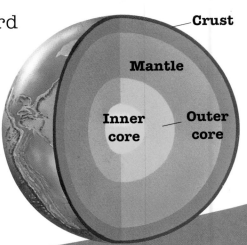

Crust

Mantle

Inner core

Outer core

CUT THROUGH THE WORLD

Make a colorful diagram, called a cross section, of Earth's insides. A cross section is like a 2-D (two-dimensional) slice cut through Earth's core.

The inner core of hard rock is very hot.

1 You will need four sheets of colored paper and a large sheet of cardboard. Use a compass to draw a dark-colored circle with a radius of 5 inches, a red circle with a radius of $4^1/_2$ inches, an orange circle with a radius of 3 inches, and a yellow circle with a radius of $1^1/_2$ inches. Cut out the circles.

Earth is like an egg, with a thin shell called the crust.

Radius

2 Glue the 5-inch circle to the cardboard. Line up all the centers of the circles. Now glue the 4$\frac{1}{2}$-inch circle on top of the 5-inch circle. Glue the 3-inch circle on top of the 4$\frac{1}{2}$-inch circle. Glue the 1$\frac{1}{2}$-inch circle down last. Label each layer and decorate each one using pencils of the same color.

The mantle, made up of hard rock and magma, is 1,900 miles thick.

The outer core is made up of liquid magma.

GOING DOWN

● The deepest hole ever drilled into the Earth's crust is in Russia and is 8 miles deep. This is nearly 3 miles deeper than Mount Everest, the world's highest mountain, is high.

● The thickness of the Earth's crust varies. Beneath the oceans, it is around 3 miles thick. Beneath continents, it can be 22 miles thick. Beneath high mountains, the crust is even thicker.

Ocean

Continental crust

Oceanic crust

Mantle

MOVING PLATES

Earth's thin crust is made up of several pieces, called tectonic plates, that move around on top of magma in the mantle. When plates collide, mountain ranges form. When they slide past each other, there is an earthquake. When they separate or move beneath the mantle, a volcano erupts. Once, all the continents were joined in a huge landmass called Pangaea. Plate movement over millions of years caused them to drift to their present positions.

JIGSAW WORLD

Some of the continent shapes you see on maps can still be fitted together like a jigsaw to make part of Pangaea.

Australia

South America

Africa

Antarctica

1 Each shape above shows a continent or part of a continent. Count the squares in the orange part of each shape, then copy the outline onto graph paper with large squares. This will give you continents of the same shape, but bigger.

2 Now copy the blue outline around each of your enlarged continents. This represents the continental shelf—the part of the seabed that the continent sits on. Continental shelves are the shallowest parts of the sea.

3 Glue the shapes onto a sheet of stiff cardboard and color them in. Make sure you color the continental shelves blue. Then carefully cut out each shape.

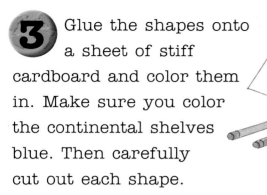

4 Piece together your jigsaw on a large tray. Look carefully at the red area on the big globe below to see what the finished jigsaw should look like.

COLLISION COURSE
● Some tectonic plates have drifted apart, but others have moved closer together. The subcontinent of India (in red below) was once farther south. It gradually moved northward until it collided with Asia. The mountains called the Himalayas were formed as the continental plates collided.

5 million years ago

135 million years ago

India

200 million years ago

Pangaea, 220 million years ago

● The plates that make up the oceanic crust also move. Here, under the ocean, the rocks are much younger. As the plates pull apart, magma rises from the mantle and solidifies to form new rock.

SHAPING MOUNTAINS

Within Earth's crust, there are layers of different rock. These layers are called strata. When moving tectonic plates collide, rock strata are forced upward and shaped into mountains with sharp peaks. These are called fold mountains. The peaks of the Himalayas are fold mountains. So are the Andes, in South America, which are several ranges of mountains formed by plate movements.

FOLDING MOUNTAINS

To make a model showing how rock strata are pushed upward to make high mountains, you will need some colored clay and a knife.

1 Roll and shape clay into strips about $1/2$ inch thick. Place the strips on top of each other and cut them to form a block of layers that look like rock strata.

2 Hold each end of your "strata" block and gently push inward. Watch the mountains fold. Make another block and repeat. See how many different mountain shapes you can make this way.

WHAT'S HAPPENING

● The force of plates colliding makes rock strata at the plate edges buckle in different ways. Sometimes rock material from one plate is squeezed against the other plate. It crumples to form more mountains.

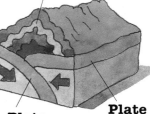

Fold mountains form as rock buckles under pressure.

Plate **Plate**

CONE-SHAPED MOUNTAINS

● Not all mountains are fold mountains. Many steep-sided mountains start as volcanoes. Over time, the lava cools and hardens into a cone shape (see page 40).

Layers of cooled lava

TRENCHES AND SEAMOUNTS

● Most oceans were formed after the breakup of Pangaea. The oceanic crust is still widening. As it collides with a continental plate, it slips below it, and a trench forms. Many tectonic plate edges lie beneath the oceans. The Marianas Trench beneath the Pacific Ocean is the deepest trench in the world, over 6 miles deep in places. Look it up in an atlas.

● As heat from inside Earth rises, huge ridges push up underwater. These undersea mountains, called seamounts, are mostly cone-shaped.

Seamounts

The ocean bed is known as the abyssal plain.

Trench

FAULTS AND EARTHQUAKES

As tectonic plates move around, rocks split and form cracks called faults. The land moves where there is a fault. Mountains with flat tops, called block mountains, form when the rock is forced up. Wide rift valleys form when the rock slips down between two faults. There is a large rift valley in East Africa. Earthquakes happen when rocks crack and move suddenly at a fault. In some parts of the world, such as Japan, this happens regularly.

BLOCK AND RIFT MODEL

To make this model, you will need a cardboard box, thin cardboard, flour, cold water, newspaper, a craft knife, tape, glue, sand, paints, and colored paper.

1 Carefully copy the shape of the model shown here onto the sides of the box. Ask an adult to help you cut around the outline with a craft knife.

2 Cover the top of the box with the cardboard. Use tape to hold it in place.

3 Mix cold water and flour to make a paste. Crumple sheets of newspaper and dip them in the paste. Lay the crumpled newspaper on the model to give the land some shape.

4 When the model is dry, paint it with a mixture of sand and paint. This will give it a textured surface. Glue strips of colored paper to the sides, as shown, to make strata.

WHAT'S HAPPENING

● Pressure pushing up from under the ground forces land upward to create block mountains. A rift valley forms if the land between two parallel faults slips downward.

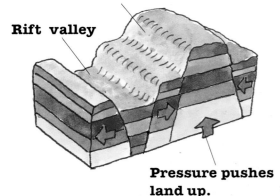

Block mountain

Rift valley

Pressure pushes land up.

EARTHQUAKES

● Earthquakes often happen at plate edges where two plates push against each other. Rocks can stand this pressure for many years, but eventually the strain becomes too great and the rocks snap into a new position. Vibrations caused by the sudden movement spread out from a point underground, called the focus, and make the ground shake.

Plates push against each other, and stress builds.

The rocks snap into place, causing an earthquake.

Epicenter

Damage is worst at the epicenter, directly above the focus.

● The Richter scale measures energy released by an earthquake on a number scale from one to nine.

Small earthquake = up to 4.5

Moderate earthquake = 4.5 - 5.5

Major earthquake = 6.5 - 7.5

Great earthquake = more than 7.5

VOLCANOES

Volcanoes are found mainly on the edges of tectonic plates. They are vents or "chimneys" in Earth's crust, through which magma from Earth's mantle erupts to the surface. On the surface, the magma cools to form lava. The lava flows in streams from the vents. Over thousands of years, the surfaces around the vents build up until mountains are formed. A volcano's shape depends on the kind of lava that erupts from it.

LOVELY LAVA

There are different kinds of lava, which flow at different speeds. Lava can be viscous (thick and sticky) like molasses or very runny.

1 Use different lavalike liquids to find out which kind travels fastest down a slope. You will need a metal tray, pancake syrup, cooking oil, and molasses.

2 Place a spoonful of each liquid at one end of the tray. Tilt the tray. Use a watch that shows seconds to time how long each liquid takes to reach the bottom of the tray. Write down the times.

3 Now see how the times differ if you warm or cool the liquids. Ask an adult to help you put the containers in hot water for a while. Then repeat step 2, noting the new flow times. Now put the containers in cool water and repeat the project.

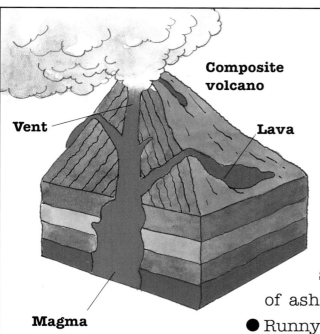

Composite volcano

Vent

Lava

Magma

VOLCANOES IN ACTION

● Viscous, cooler lava flows more slowly than hot, runny lava. Composite volcanoes have steep sides because they are formed by repeated and frequent flows of stiff, viscous lava. Volcanic eruptions from cones like these are extremely violent.

● Cinder volcanoes are also steep-sided, but are formed by layers of ash and cinder rather than lava.

● Runny lava erupts more gently, then spreads out. Shield and fissure volcanoes form this way.

GEYSERS

● Underground water is sometimes heated by hot magma, and geysers of hot water shoot up out of the ground. These are used as sources of geothermal energy in countries like Iceland.

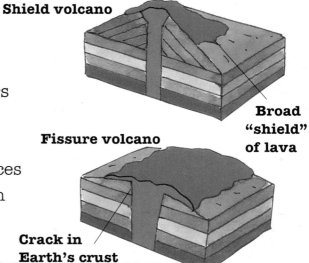

Shield volcano

Broad "shield" of lava

Fissure volcano

Crack in Earth's crust

ROCKS AND MINERALS

The oldest rocks, called igneous rocks, contain crystals. Once igneous rocks have been broken down and changed by the weather, they become sedimentary, or secondhand, rocks. Fossils can be found in the layers, or strata, of sedimentary rocks. Under certain conditions, sedimentary rock can change into another, harder kind of rock, called metamorphic rock.

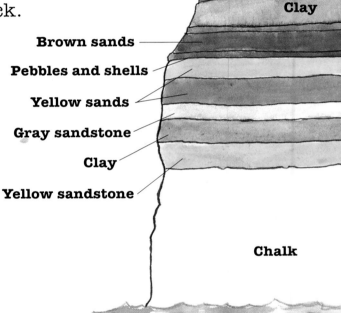

Soil and grass

Clay

Brown sands

Pebbles and shells

Yellow sands

Gray sandstone

Clay

Yellow sandstone

Chalk

Granite (igneous)

Sandstone (sedimentary)

Marble (metamorphic)

SEDIMENT

To create your own sedimentary layers, you will need some gravel, sand, and mud, a jar with a lid, and some water.

● Igneous rocks, like granite, are being formed all the time inside the Earth. Sedimentary rocks, like sandstone, are worn-down igneous rocks. Immense heat and pressure can transform a sedimentary rock, like limestone, into a metamorphic rock, like marble.

1 Put equal amounts of sand, gravel, and mud in layers inside the jar. Cover the layers with water.

2 Screw on the lid tightly, then shake the contents of the jar. Leave it to settle for a few days. Layers of sediment will form.

3 Look closely at the layers. The material with the largest grains settles to the bottom of the jar. Smaller-grained material comes to the top. Make drawings of your "strata" and label them, as in the drawing opposite.

WHERE MINERALS COME FROM

● Rocks are made of minerals. Diamonds are minerals. They are the hardest material known and are used to make cutting tools.

● A scale called Mohs' scale is used to grade the hardness of minerals. Diamonds are at the top of the scale at 10. A mineral at one level can cut minerals in any lower level. Topaz, at 8, is two places below diamond.

Topaz

Diamond

● Diamonds form when magma pushes up volcanic vents and solidifies under great heat and pressure. As it cools, crystals of pure carbon form inside the rock. These carbon crystals are diamonds. Slow cooling makes the largest crystals. As the rock breaks down, some diamond crystals come to the surface.

Some crystals are washed down to the sea.

Volcanic vent

MOUNTAINS AND MAPS

To design maps, cartographers (mapmakers) need exact measurements of the land. Surveyors measure and calculate land height using an instrument called a theodolite. This means that maps can be drawn to scale and can show the exact shape of the land. Mountain heights are always measured from sea level.

1 Ask an adult to help you score the cardboard diagonally using a ruler and craft knife. Cut it in half to make two right-angled triangles. Use only one half.

60°
30°
90°

MOUNTAIN MEASURE

To make and use a theodolite, you need a tape measure, a rectangle of stiff cardboard, a small cardboard tube, thread, tape, a ruler, a craft knife, and string with a key attached.

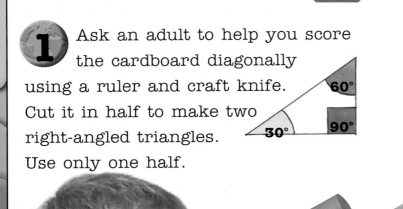

2 Cut the cardboard tube in half to make two viewers for your theodolite. To make "sights," tape two pieces of thread across the viewing end of each tube, as shown here. Make sure they cross in the center.

3 Tape a viewer to each end of the long side of the triangle. Make a hole at the top of the short side. Push the free end of the string with the key on it through the hole, then knot it so that the key hangs down. This is your plumb line.

HELPFUL HINTS
● Test your theodolite by trying it out on something you already know the height of. You may need to walk backward or forward until you can line up the viewers with the top of the object being measured.

4 Now look through the viewers and line up the center of the sights with the top of a tree. Move forward or backward until the plumb line hangs straight down along the short side of the triangle.

(b)

(a)

5 Ask a friend to measure the distance between you and the foot of the tree (a). The height of the tree is that distance added to your own height (b).

SPOT HEIGHTS AND CONTOURS
● On a contour map, lines join points at the same height above sea level. Where contour lines are very close together, it means the land rises steeply. The highest point on a hill or mountain cannot be shown by contour lines. Instead, a spot height is written on the map showing the exact height at that point. Look in an atlas to find the exact height of Mount Everest.

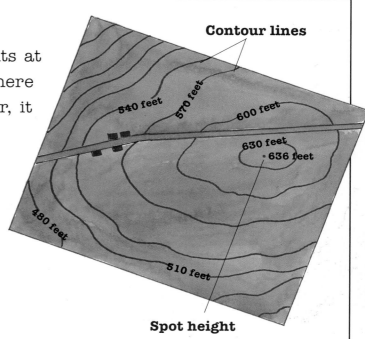

Contour lines

540 feet

570 feet

600 feet

630 feet

· 636 feet

480 feet

510 feet

Spot height

HOW HIGH?

Altitude means height above sea level. At high altitudes, the air is thin because there is less oxygen in the Earth's atmosphere at that level. People born in high places have a large heart and lungs, and wide nostrils to breathe in more oxygen. The weight of air pressing down on Earth, called air pressure, is low at high altitudes. In the same way, water pressure is low near the surface (the top) of the sea.

Everest—29,028 feet

Kilimanjaro—19,341 feet

Ben Nevis—4,406 feet

PRESSURE BOTTLE

Make a fountain to show water pressure at work. Air pressure works the same way. You need an empty plastic bottle, a tray, a funnel, clay, paper, a compass, glue, and colored pencils.

1 Look in an atlas to find out the heights of three high mountains. Chart the heights on a picture graph, as shown. Glue the chart around the plastic bottle, leaving a gap down one side.

2 Use a compass to make three holes in the bottle. Position the holes vertically (one above the other) in the gap on the bottle. Make each hole level with the highest point of one of the mountains on your chart.

3 Before filling the plastic bottle with water, cover all three holes with clay. Make sure each hole is completely watertight.

4 Stand the bottle on a tray. Use a funnel to fill the bottle to the top with water. Carefully remove the three pieces of clay and watch what happens.

WHAT'S HAPPENING

● You will notice that the fountain of water at the top does not spurt as far as the two beneath. This is because water pressure is lower at the top than at the bottom. There is more water pushing down on the water at the bottom of the bottle than on the water at the top. In the same way, air pressure is lower at the top of a mountain than at the bottom.

CLEAR AIR

● Astronomers prefer to place telescopes at the tops of mountains because of the thinner, clearer air there. There are few clouds at high altitudes, which makes it much easier to see the stars and planets.

ICE AND SNOW

The higher you go, the colder the climate. Snow is found on mountain peaks, even close to the equator. The level above which snow lies permanently is called the snow line. At the North Pole and South Pole, the snow line is at sea level. Ice forms beneath heavy snow, and rivers of ice called glaciers move slowly down mountainsides carving U-shaped valleys.

HOT WIRE

To show how ice can slide over rocky surfaces, as a glacier does, you will need an ice tray, a freezer, two supports, wire, a large tray, and weights.

1 Fill a rectangular ice tray with water and freeze it. Remove your long ice cube from the dish and position it across the supports, like a bridge, on a large tray.

2 Ask an adult to help you make a wire sling to hold the weights, as shown. Loop a length of wire around the ice cube, and attach its ends to the sling. The sling should hang straight down but not touch the tray.

3 Watch the wire as the heavy weights drag it slowly through the ice. The wire cuts through the ice, but the ice remains in one piece. Eventually, the wire will pass through the ice completely.

WHAT'S HAPPENING

● The pressure of the weighted wire melts the ice, letting the wire pass through it. But above the wire there is no pressure, so the ice freezes again. Below glaciers, the same thing happens as moving ice meets a large rock. The ice melts, flows around the rock, and freezes again on the other side. Melting and refreezing helps the ice slide over large obstacles.

Wire

MOVING ICE AND SNOW

● Glaciers can move around large rocks, but they pick up loose pieces of rock and carry them down mountainsides. These rocks wear away the ground beneath to form U-shaped valleys and also bowl-shaped hollows near mountain peaks, called corries, or cirques.

● When heavy snow slides down a mountainside, it is called an avalanche. Avalanches often happen when the ground warms slightly and the first snowfall does not freeze hard. A loud noise, or skiers, can set off an avalanche. Whole villages can be buried under the snow.

U-shaped valley

The fjords in Norway were formed by glaciers.

Loose snow

RAIN SHADOW

Rain falls when warm, moist winds blow from the sea, reach land, then are forced to rise and cool over high mountaintops. Moisture in cooling air near mountain peaks condenses (turns into tiny droplets) to form clouds. When the clouds can hold no more moisture, rain falls. This is called orographic, or relief, rainfall. The far side of the mountain, called the lee side, remains dry, with no rainfall. It is said to be in the rain shadow of the mountain.

WHERE DID ALL THE RAIN GO?

Choose a very rainy day to observe the rain shadow beside a wall. You will need waterproof clothing, three containers (all the same shape and size), and a ruler.

Altitude increases

1 Wearing waterproofs, position one container right beside a wall, and the other two containers at varying distances from it. As soon as the rain stops, bring the containers indoors. Be careful not to mix them up!

2 Measure the amount of water in each container. You should find that the container that was nearest the wall has the least water in it. The wall creates a rain shadow. Look at the ground near the wall. Does it seem drier than elsewhere?

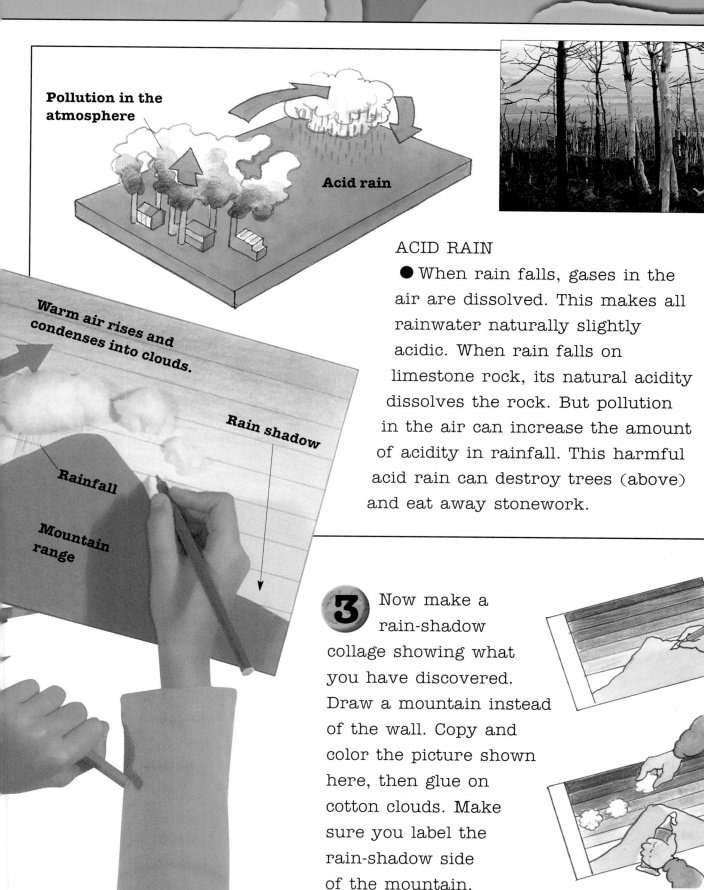

Pollution in the atmosphere

Acid rain

Warm air rises and condenses into clouds.

Rain shadow

Rainfall

Mountain range

ACID RAIN
● When rain falls, gases in the air are dissolved. This makes all rainwater naturally slightly acidic. When rain falls on limestone rock, its natural acidity dissolves the rock. But pollution in the air can increase the amount of acidity in rainfall. This harmful acid rain can destroy trees (above) and eat away stonework.

3 Now make a rain-shadow collage showing what you have discovered. Draw a mountain instead of the wall. Copy and color the picture shown here, then glue on cotton clouds. Make sure you label the rain-shadow side of the mountain.

EROSION AND WEATHERING

Over time, land is worn away by rivers and seas, and also by weather. This is called erosion. The eroded material is carried away and left somewhere else. This is called deposition. Erosion and deposition always happen together. On mountain slopes, ice, wind, frost, and rain wear away the rock. Water collects in cracks, freezes, and causes the rock to break. Loose banks of stones may slide down slopes, forming screes.

CRACKING UP

Using balls of modeling clay rolled in plastic wrap, you can carry out an experiment that shows why and how mountain rocks are eroded by frost and ice.

2 Freeze one of the balls of clay. Leave it in the freezer for 24 hours, then remove it. Let it thaw out completely. Then remove the plastic wrap. What differences do you notice between the two balls of clay? Look at the cracks in the thawed clay.

1 Roll two balls from damp modeling clay in the palm of your hands. Spray the outside of the clay with water. Then wrap each ball separately in plastic wrap.

MUDSLIDES

- The clearing of trees from land is called deforestation. Mountainsides erode more quickly after people have chopped down trees. Soil on bare slopes is easily washed away by rain because tree roots no longer hold the soil in place. Heavy rain on eroded slopes can cause mudslides that destroy roads and bury whole towns.

WHAT'S HAPPENING

- Eventually your frozen clay will shatter. The experiment has reproduced what happens, again and again, to rocks frozen by ice and frost on a mountain. Imagine rocks frozen many, many times over centuries. Eventually, those rocks crack, and stones roll down the slopes to form screes.

- The clay shatters because ice fills more space than water, so ice in a crack pushes against the sides and opens the crack even farther. Test this by filling a plastic bottle three-quarters full and freezing it. The ice will fill the bottle—or even break out of it!

3 Spray the thawed clay again. Cover it again with plastic wrap and refreeze. Remove after 24 hours and carry out another observation. Repeat this two or three times, and note the changes each time.

CHAPTER 3
Rivers and Seas

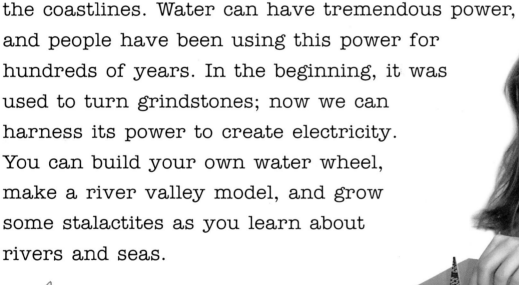

In this chapter, you can find out where rivers are formed, and how they cut their way through the land, forming valleys, waterfalls, and lakes on their way. Ocean tides and waves also change the shape of the land along the coastlines. Water can have tremendous power, and people have been using this power for hundreds of years. In the beginning, it was used to turn grindstones; now we can harness its power to create electricity. You can build your own water wheel, make a river valley model, and grow some stalactites as you learn about rivers and seas.

CONTENTS

THE SAME WATER

Almost three-quarters of the Earth's surface is water. Most of it is in our oceans or frozen in glaciers (see page 49). In warm weather, water evaporates from rivers and seas, which means it changes into an invisible gas called water vapor. When water vapor cools, it condenses, becomes water again, and falls as rain. This is called the water cycle. The amount of water around us stays the same—it just keeps moving through the water cycle.

WATER CYCLE

Make a model to show the water cycle in action. You will need two large plastic bottles, a narrow cardboard box, a craft knife, cardboard, a wire coat hanger, glue, sticky tape, paint, an aluminum foil tray, ice cubes, and hot water. Ask an adult to help you with the cutting, shaping of hooks, and pouring hot water.

1 Draw the outline of a tree-covered mountain slope on one side of the box. Cut around the shape. Paint the outside of the box.

2 Cut a plastic bottle in half lengthwise. Glue one half inside the box to make a river valley. Slide the foil "sea" tray into the box beneath the narrow end of the bottle.

3 Cut the neck off another large plastic bottle. Cut cloud shapes from cardboard and glue them to one side of the bottle.

OCEAN DEPTHS
● The largest ocean in the world is the Pacific Ocean. An iron ball dropped into the deepest part, which is over 6 miles deep, would take an hour to reach the ocean floor.

N. America

Pacific Ocean

Australia

4 Make hooks from a coat hanger and tape them to the other side of the box, as shown. Rest the bottle on the hooks with its open end facing outward. It should dip at a slight angle.

WHAT'S HAPPENING

● Your model demonstrates what happens in the real water cycle, shown here.

5 Put ice cubes into the suspended bottle. Pour hot water into the foil tray. Watch the water vapor rise to make "rain" fall from the cloud.

3. The wind blows the clouds toward high land, where the moist air rises and cools even more.

2. As it rises, the water vapor cools and condenses to form tiny droplets, which form clouds.

4. The clouds burst and rain falls into rivers, which flow back to the sea.

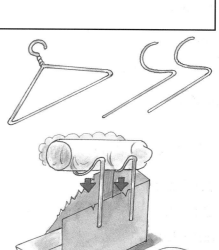

1. Heat from the Sun evaporates water from seas and rivers.

5. Some rainwater seeps through the land.

FROM SOURCE TO MOUTH

Rivers begin in the mountains. Some start from a melting glacier or lake. Others start as underground springs. Mountain streams are fast-flowing. They erode (carve out) deep V-shaped valleys. As they reach lower land, closer to the sea, rivers flow more slowly. Here, they erode U-shaped valleys as they curve across wide, flat areas of land called floodplains. The natural loop-like curves shaped by a river are called meanders.

MEANDERING AROUND

To show how water likes to meander, you will need sand, a shallow tray, a ruler, a plastic plant trough, wooden blocks, and a pitcher of water.

1 Scoop dry sand into the tray until it is full. Use the ruler, as shown here, to level the surface and remove any extra sand. Make sure the surface is even.

2 Arrange the blocks so that they are higher than the edge of the plant trough. Position the sand-filled tray with one end on the blocks and the other on the edge of the plant trough. Make sure the tray is sloping gently down toward the trough.

3 Gently pour water onto the sand, so that it flows evenly down the slope. Keep pouring steadily. Watch as your "river" changes its course.

WHAT'S HAPPENING

● All rivers make meanders. Meanders curve more as rivers flow over flat floodplains.

● Water flows faster on outside curves and this erodes the river bank. Where the river flow is slower, on inside curves, material that has been carried down the river is deposited (laid down).

Flow is faster and deeper on outside curves. Cliffs form as river banks are eroded.

If a meander becomes too tightly curved, the river flows across the neck of the curve, leaving an oxbow lake.

Flow is slower and shallower on inside curves. Shoals or sand bars form as material is deposited.

Old course of river

Meander

A delta is the low-lying fan-shaped area at the mouth of the river.

Braiding happens where a river becomes a mass of channels. Temporary islands appear. Flooding changes the shape of braiding.

Lip

WATERFALLS

● Where rivers flow over bands of rock that are too hard to be eroded, a waterfall forms. These can be a few feet high, forming rapids, or hundreds of feet high. On high waterfalls, the water spills over the rock at the lip. A deep pool, called a plunge pool, is eroded by rocks and pebbles that swirl around at the base of a high waterfall.

Plunge pool

UNDERGROUND WATER

Water not carried away by rivers becomes ground water. It seeps through cracks and pores (tiny holes) in rocks and collects underground. Rock that soaks up water like a sponge, like sandstone, is called porous rock. Other rock, like limestone, has many cracks and joints for water to seep through. When rainwater, which is slightly acidic, soaks through limestone, it dissolves minerals in the rock and eventually carves out an underground cave. Inside, "icicles" of rock, called stalactites and stalagmites, form from dissolved minerals.

GROWING STALACTITES

Grow some stalactites using a saturated solution of baking soda (see step 1), two jars, a dish, two paper clips, and some yarn.

1 Fill each jar with warm water. Add baking soda to the water and stir. Keep adding soda until no more can be dissolved. This is a saturated solution.

2 Place the jars slightly apart, in a very warm place, with a dish between them. Fasten a paper clip to each end of the yarn. Lower a paper clip into each jar, as shown, so that the yarn hangs over the dish.

3 Now watch the slow growth of a stalactite in the center of the yarn—it will take about a week for a good stalactite to form. Keep a note of how much it grows each day.

WHAT'S HAPPENING

● The soda solution seeps upward, then collects and drips from the center of the yarn. As the water in the solution evaporates, the soda deposit remains and a stalactite grows down from the yarn.

● Stalactites hang down from cave ceilings. Stalagmites build up from the ground. If you leave it long enough, a stalagmite will grow from the water that drips onto the dish.

FLOODING

● Rainwater can seep only so far into the ground. The level at which it stops, where the rock is saturated (can absorb no more water), is called the water table.

● Limestone is permeable rock— it lets rainwater soak through its cracks until the ground beneath is saturated.

Limestone

Water table

In frequent heavy rain, limestone areas are likely to flood as the water seeps through the rock and raises the level of the water table.

● Heavy rain in mountains is carried downstream in rivers, so floods often happen on floodplains. People build defenses, called levees, to protect their homes.

Floodplain

Major flood level

Flood level
Average river level

Levee

DOWNRIVER

Settlements are often built close to rivers. In the desert area of North Africa, the Nile River provides water for farmers, who grow crops along its banks. The Nile begins as two tributaries, the Blue Nile and the White Nile, which join, then flow northward into the Mediterranean Sea. The Nile is the world's longest river. It is over 4,000 miles long, which is farther than the distance from New York to London.

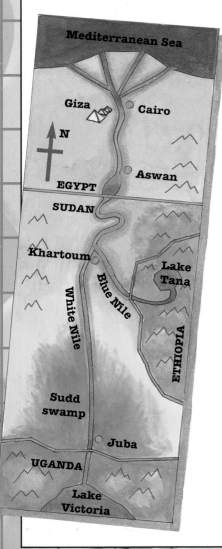

NILE MODEL

A linear map (left) shows important landmarks along a river valley. To make a model of the Nile using this linear map, use a large board, flour, water, newspaper, cardboard, sand, paint, and bottle tops.

Use bottle tops for towns and cities.

1 Find the Nile in an atlas. See if you can spot all the landmarks shown on the linear map. The linear map has no scale. This means that it gives the names of places, but does not show true distance.

2 To make your model, first draw the shape of the Nile onto the board. Then paint it blue. Paint the fertile fields along the river banks green.

3 To make mountains, mix flour and cold water into a thick paste. Tear newspaper into small pieces and soak these in the paste to make papier-mâché. Position small mounds of papier-mâché on the board and shape them into peaks.

Mix sand with yellow paint for the desert.

Make pyramids from cardboard.

When your papier-mâché peaks are dry, paint them.

4 When the painted model is dry, use bottle tops and cardboard to mark the positions of any landmarks, like towns and pyramids. Look at the linear map to find their names, then write neat labels for them.

CROSSING RIVERS

● The first bridge was probably a fallen tree laid across a stream. Now, engineers decide which kind of bridge to build by studying the weight it has to carry and the width of the river.

Suspension bridges are used to span wide rivers or bays. They are supported by cables made from strong steel wires twisted together.

Weight on bridge

Weight spread

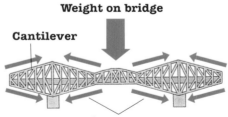

Weight on bridge

Cantilever

Weight spread

A **cantilever bridge** is a balanced structure. Separate cantilevers are joined by short spans of steel.

An **arched bridge** is a very strong structure, as it spreads weight outward and downward around the whole length of each arch.

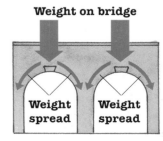

Weight on bridge

Weight spread

Weight spread

RIVER POLLUTION

At its source in the mountains, a stream is sparkling and clear, but farther downstream, human activities cause pollution that reduces the oxygen in the water. Fresh water can become so polluted that plants and animals die. Pesticides sprayed on crops are washed into rivers by the rain.

Trash is often dumped in rivers. Waste materials from factories and mines are piped into rivers.

MUDDY FILTER

Our drinking water comes from the water in the water cycle. It is filtered and purified before it reaches our faucets. You can make a water filter using a plastic bottle, sand, water, soil, a paper coffee filter, and a pitcher.

1 Ask an adult to cut the top from the plastic bottle about 4 inches from the lid. Place the top upside down, inside the bottle. Tap it firmly into place.

2 Position the filter paper inside the bottle top. Spoon a layer of sand into the filter. Pour enough water onto the sand to make it wet.

3 Mix soil and water in the pitcher. Slowly pour the muddy mixture onto the wet sand inside the filter. Watch the water pass through the sand and collect in the bottom of the bottle.

4 Now study the water in the bottom of the bottle. It will look cleaner, but beware, it is not fit to drink! Our drinking water is filtered many times before it comes out of the faucet. Compare your filtered water with tap water to see the difference.

POLLUTION DISASTERS

● The Rhine is the longest and dirtiest river in Europe. In 1986, after a fire at the Sandoz factory in Switzerland, more than 30 tons of chemicals entered the Rhine (see right). For 125 miles downstream, all living things in the river died. In January 2000, pollution of the Tisza River in Hungary killed most of the fish within hours.

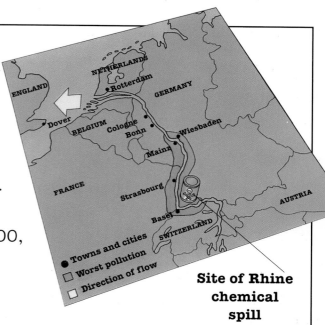

Site of Rhine chemical spill

ENGLAND

NETHERLANDS
Rotterdam

GERMANY

Dover

BELGIUM
Cologne
Bonn

Wiesbaden

Mainz

FRANCE

Strasbourg

Basel

AUSTRIA

SWITZERLAND

● Towns and cities
□ Worst pollution
□ Direction of flow

OXYGEN IN WATER

● Water creatures need oxygen to survive. Much oxygen is released from water plants during photosynthesis, which is the way that plants make food using sunlight. You can test this by putting some Canadian pondweed in a bowl of water. Stand it in the Sun and watch bubbles of oxygen appear.

TOO WET, TOO DRY?

In arid (dry) parts of the world, rain may not fall for months. Rivers stop flowing and soil becomes too dry to grow crops. Farmers need to irrigate their land, which means they supply water to the fields, often through ditches. The ancient Egyptians used an irrigation device called a *shaduf*, which is still used today. Tropical countries have a dry and a wet season. In the wet season, there are sudden, heavy downpours. Sometimes there are floods and drought in the same year.

RAISING WATER

To see how a *shaduf* works, you need a craft knife, corrugated cardboard, tape, a clean yogurt cup, string, a wooden spoon, and clay.

1 Ask an adult to help you cut and fold a strip of corrugated cardboard as shown below. Cut a slot at each end, wide enough for the handle of your wooden spoon.

Fold

2 Tie a long piece of string around the yogurt cup under the rim, as shown, then over the top to make a big loop.

3 Knot another piece of string onto the loop on the cup and tie the other end to the wooden spoon, as shown. Tape a large lump of clay to the spoon.

4 Slot and tape the spoon into the base, toward the clay end, as shown. You may have to add more clay when the bucket is full of water, so that it swings up easily.

5 Place your *shaduf* beside a full sink or basin. Lower the bucket. When it is full, you should be able to raise it very easily by the string. You can now pour the water into another basin.

WHAT'S HAPPENING

● A *shaduf* works as a lever. The clay weight makes it easy to lift the full bucket. In Egypt, water is raised from the Nile and poured into channels to irrigate the fields.

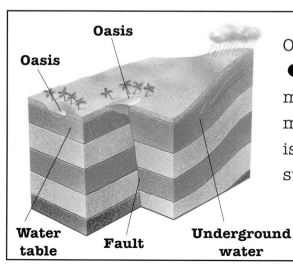

OASIS

● Underground water can seep hundreds of miles through the water table, from distant mountains to low-lying areas. An oasis is where the water table emerges at the surface. This can happen at a hollow in the sand or at a fault, where rock has moved suddenly and a spring appears.

Oasis
Oasis
Oasis
Water table
Fault
Underground water

THE POWER OF WATER

Water power is a clean, renewable source of energy. It has been used for hundreds of years to do work. Water wheels once turned grindstones. Now, water turbines are harnessed to generators that make electricity. This is called hydroelectric power. Huge dams have been built across rivers to provide electricity for cities and towns. However, large dams cause damage to the surrounding land and many people now believe that small dams are better.

WATER WHEEL

To make a water wheel, you will need two large plastic lids, glue, craft sticks, a tray, a craft knife, a plastic bottle, paint, a pushpin, doweling, cardboard, a pitcher, a compass, and water.

1 Ask an adult to pierce a hole in the top of each of the two lids. Glue them together as shown. Now glue craft sticks around the edge of the lids to make paddles.

2 Ask an adult to cut V-shapes in the cardboard. Score and fold the cardboard and position around the tray, as shown, to make a support.

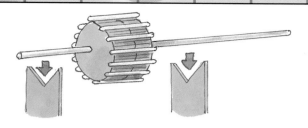

3 Push the doweling through the holes in your wheel, so that one end sticks out farther than the other. Rest it inside the V-shaped notches, as shown.

4 Use a compass to draw a flywheel on cardboard. Cut it out and color brightly. Push a pushpin through the center of the flywheel and into the long end of the doweling.

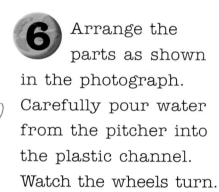

5 Ask an adult to cut sections from the bottle and glue them together, as shown. Make another support, this time with U-shaped notches and one end higher than the other. Glue on the plastic.

6 Arrange the parts as shown in the photograph. Carefully pour water from the pitcher into the plastic channel. Watch the wheels turn.

WHAT'S HAPPENING

● The energy of the falling water turns the wheel, which spins the flywheel. Raise the pitcher higher, and the added energy in the water will make the wheel turn faster.

● Your flywheel represents a turbine, which drives a generator.

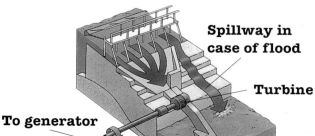

Spillway in case of flood

Turbine

To generator

TIDAL POWER

● Energy from the sea is also used to make electricity. The tide comes in and goes out twice daily. Power stations built across estuaries use turbines that spin in two directions, to harness the tide's energy both as it comes in and as it goes out.

ON THE BEACH

The sea's tides and crashing waves change the shape of our coasts. Tides are caused mainly by the pull of the Moon as it circles the Earth. The pull makes oceans on each side of the globe bulge a little (a high tide) and then fall back (a low tide) every 12 hours or so. Pounding waves and the material they carry cause erosion and deposition. These work together to break down and build up our beaches and cliffs, sometimes forming rocky arches and stacks.

MAKE A COASTLINE

Build a model coastline with a sandy beach to show how waves can gradually wash away the sand from our beaches and form stacks.

1 You will need a long waterproof tray, a pitcher, modeling clay, sand, water, and cardboard. First, shape some tall clay rock stacks and press them firmly in place toward one end of the tray, as shown here.

2 Fill about half the tray with sand, making sure the clay stacks are completely covered. Gently pour water into the rest of the tray.

WHAT'S HAPPENING

● When a part of a wave hits shallower water, it slows down and the rest of the wave bends. When waves reach a headland, they slow, swing around the headland, and hit its sides. This gradually wears it away, leaving a stack or arch.

Headland

Wave direction

Waves bend

Stack formed from old headland

Spit

LONGSHORE DRIFT

● Waves curve and hit bays at an angle. This carries pebbles and sand diagonally up the beach. The wave backwash pulls the pebbles and sand back down the slope at right angles to the beach, gradually moving them along in a series of zigzag patterns. This is called longshore drift. Sand banks and spits are formed this way.

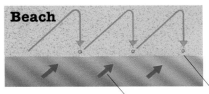

Beach

Sand particle

Wave direction

PEBBLES

● Pebbles are rocks worn smooth by attrition (rubbing against each other) in rivers or seas. They may be flat or rounded, but are always smooth. Shake sugar lumps in a jar. Watch the edges of the cubes rub against each other until they are smooth, like pebbles.

3 Move the cardboard back and forth to make waves. Gradually, the movement of the waves will wash away, or erode, the sand and expose the stacks. You may even see an arch forming between stacks.

WAVES AND WIND

Waves are started by the wind, way out at sea. It whips the water surface into ripples, which build up into waves as the wind gets stronger. The waves get bigger and bigger as they travel through the sea. Although the waves travel great distances, the water in them stays in the same place, moving up and down, until the wave hits a coast. A huge wave called a tsunami can form if there is an underwater earthquake.

TESTING THE WIND

The stronger the wind, the bigger the wave. Test wind strength by building an anemometer. You will need cardboard, a ping-pong ball, a compass, a pen, a ruler, a craft knife, a pushpin, and glue.

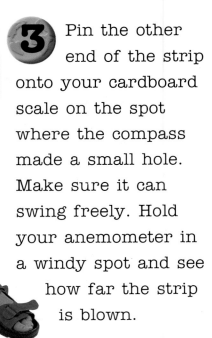

1 Use the compass to draw a curve onto the cardboard. Mark off equal spaces, making a scale for comparing wind speeds.

2 Ask an adult to cut a strip of cardboard with a window, so that you can see the scale. Glue the ping-pong ball to one end.

3 Pin the other end of the strip onto your cardboard scale on the spot where the compass made a small hole. Make sure it can swing freely. Hold your anemometer in a windy spot and see how far the strip is blown.

WAVE MOVEMENT

● If you throw a stone into a pond, ripples form on the surface. A boat will move up and down on the ripples, but not forward or backward. Waves at sea are the same as ripples—they don't move the water forward, only up and down.

● Beneath the waves, water particles move up and down in circles. This causes waves to turn over or break at the surface. When a wave reaches shore, it cannot circulate as well in the shallow water, so it piles up, taller and taller, until it spills over and breaks.

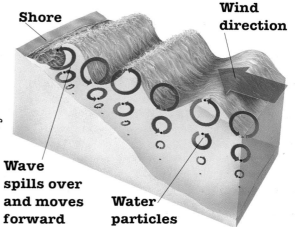

Shore

Wind direction

Wave spills over and moves forward

Water particles

BEAUFORT SCALE

● Storms at sea can drown fishermen and sailors. The Beaufort wind scale (right) was designed for sailors in 1805 by Admiral Sir Francis Beaufort. It ranges from 0 to 12, from calm to hurricane. Force 8 is a gale, force 10 is a stormy sea. Sailors and fishermen listen to the radio for gale warnings before going out to sea.

1

No wind

2

Smoke moves

4

Branches move

6

Crests on water

7

Trees bend

8

Hard to walk

10

Trees uprooted

12

Devastation

OUT AT SEA

Water in the world's oceans is moved around by ocean currents. Near the surface, these currents are caused by prevailing winds, which means winds that occur frequently in certain places. The shape of the land and the ocean floor affect deeper ocean currents. The sea water's temperature and density (the heaviness of a certain amount of water) also affect currents. Very salty water, found in hot, subtropical oceans, is more dense than less salty water, found in cold, polar oceans.

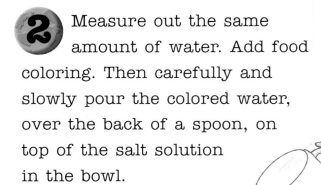

FLOATING FISH

To show that salt makes water more dense, you will need a transparent bowl, salt, a spoon, water, a potato, a pitcher, scissors, plastic lids, and food coloring.

1 Make a solution of salt by adding salt to a pitcher of water until no more will dissolve (about 12 big spoonfuls). Make a note of the amount of water you use. Pour the salt solution into the bowl.

2 Measure out the same amount of water. Add food coloring. Then carefully and slowly pour the colored water, over the back of a spoon, on top of the salt solution in the bowl.

3 Ask an adult to cut a slice of potato about 1/2 inch thick. Cut out two fins from the plastic lids and attach them to the potato body of your fish. Place the fish in the water and watch what it does.

WHAT'S HAPPENING
● The fish will sink, then float at the level of the salt water. This is because the density of the fish is less than the density of the salt water, but more than the density of the fresh water.

Fresh water

Salt water

OCEAN CURRENTS
● Currents move in circular patterns and are sometimes called gyres. In the northern hemisphere, they spin clockwise. In the southern hemisphere, they spin counterclockwise. Some currents are warm and some cold. Ocean currents warm or cool the air above them and this has a major effect on the Earth's weather.

Icy arctic currents meet warm currents from the south

Warm currents

Cold currents

EL NIÑO
● El Niño is an unusually warm current that affects the Pacific Ocean every few years, around Christmastime. It can affect weather all over the world, and is thought to have been responsible for severe droughts in southern Africa, floods in California, and hurricanes in the Atlantic.

Warm water of El Niño moves toward South America

UNDER THE SEA

The gently sloping part of the seabed around the continents is called the continental shelf. It is covered by shallow seas, but is really part of the continent. Sands and gravel in the continental shelf are rich in minerals. A large part of the world's oil and gas deposits are also found under the sea. Oil and gas are fossil fuels, formed over millions of years in layers of sedimentary rock (see page 42). They are found where silt or sand settled on the seabed and buried plant or animal remains. The world's fossil fuels are nonrenewable, which means they will eventually run out.

1. Dead sea plants and animals are buried in sediment that hardens into porous rock.

2. Over years, pressure and heat act on the rock.

They convert the dead plants and animals into oil and gas.

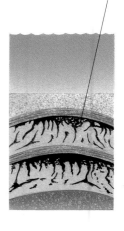

3. Underground pressure forces the oil and gas upward through the porous rock.

FOSSIL FUEL MODEL

Make a model that shows how fossil fuels are formed. You will need glue, cardboard, scissors, sand, and paint.

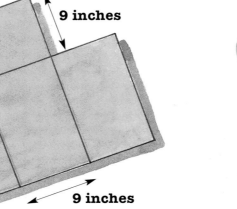

9 inches

13 inches

9 inches

1 Draw the pattern shown here on cardboard. Ask an adult to help you score, cut, and fold it into a long box shape.

2 Paint your box with the layers of sea, rock, gas, and oil shown below. Spread on some glue, then sprinkle on sand to create a realistic effect. Draw and cut out a model oil rig and glue it in position over the oil.

6. Oil rigs drill down to the reservoirs and pump up the oil.

4. The oil and gas reach nonporous rock, which they can't pass through.

5. The trapped oil (black) and gas (green) form underground pockets called reservoirs.

GLOBAL WARMING

● Burning nonrenewable fossil fuels releases polluting gases such as carbon dioxide into the air. World temperatures are thought to be rising because these gases, known as greenhouse gases, are trapping too much heat inside the Earth's atmosphere. This environmental problem is called global warming.

Heat trapped

Greenhouse gases

Heat from the Sun

● Too much global warming will melt the polar icecaps and cause sea levels around the world to rise, flooding low-lying coastal areas. The problem could be reduced if cleaner, renewable sources of energy, like water and wind, were used instead of fossil fuels.

POLLUTION AT SEA

The population of the world is now more than six billion. More people means more trash. Our oceans are now becoming dumping grounds. Polluted water is destroying the food chains of the sea. Oil tanker disasters devastate vast areas of our seas and coasts and kill or harm many thousands of birds, sea mammals, and fish. Scientists use various ways of dealing with the oil spillages. One is to disperse (break up) the oil using chemicals.

OILY WATER

Make some "slick" pictures to see how oil floats and how it can be broken up. You will need a bowl, plastic cups, oil-based paints, turpentine, water, paper, a stick, and dish detergent.

2 Fill the bowl with water. Pour in your paints and stir with a stick to make an oily "slick."

1 Ask an adult to help you mix a few drops of oil-based paint with a little turpentine in a cup. Mix several different colors.

3 Lower a sheet of paper onto the water. Let it soak up the paint, then remove and leave it to dry. Stir the water, then repeat to get different oily patterns.

4 Now squeeze a little dish detergent onto the oily paint, move the stick through it, and watch the "slick" disperse.

WHAT'S HAPPENING

● Oil is less dense than water, which means it floats on top of the water. The detergent splits the oily layer into tiny droplets, which can then sink to mix with the water below.

OIL DISASTERS

● When the oil tanker *Erika* sank off the coast of France in 1999, over 18,000 sea birds with feathers coated in oil were picked up from the oil-covered beaches. In 1989, the *Exxon Valdez* (right) hit rocks off Alaska, spilling nearly 40,000 tons of oil. It polluted 1,200 miles of coastline, killing up to 300,000 sea birds, 5,000 rare sea otters, and many seals and fish.

Exxon Valdez

ALASKA

■ **Damaged shoreline**

■ **Sea bird habitat**

□ **Sea otter habitat**

CORAL REEF DESTRUCTION

● Coral reefs are underwater ridges formed by tiny creatures called polyps. They are only found in warm, tropical seas and are home to an amazing variety of marine life. Coral reefs need crystal-clear water to survive. One-tenth of the world's coral reefs have now been so badly damaged by pollution that they will never recover.

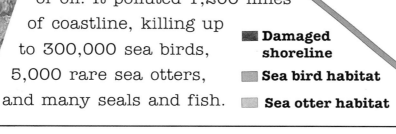

CHAPTER 4
Ecosystems

An ecosystem can be as small as an oak tree, or as large as a forest. Weather and climate play a part in every ecosystem. But not only natural factors have an impact. Human progress is forcing wildlife to adapt to change as the homes of many animals are being destroyed.

Plants and animals in a food chain depend upon each other for survival. The loss of even one species can cause damage to the entire food chain. In this chapter, you can play an ecosystem card game, make a minirainforest, and build a model food web. Learn about ecosystems so that you can help wildlife survive and flourish!

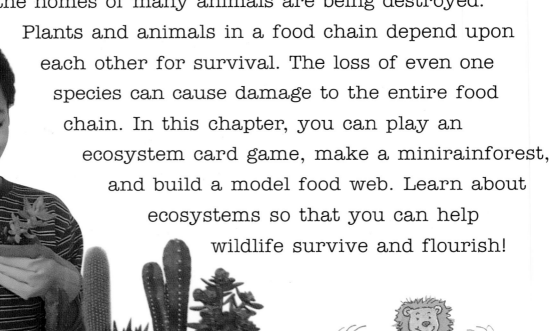

CONTENTS

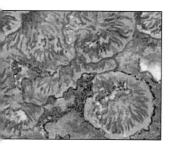

WHAT IS AN ECOSYSTEM?

The natural home of a plant or animal is called its habitat. Each habitat supports a different community (group) of living things. An ecosystem is made up of any given habitat and its community. The living things in an ecosystem interact with each other. They also interact with the nonliving parts of their environment (surroundings), such as water or weather. Ecosystems can be large or small. A pond or even a tree is a small ecosystem. Our planet is one huge ecosystem. The study of ecosystems is called ecology.

LOCAL ECOSYSTEMS

Make a local ecosystems map.
If you can, choose an area with buildings and open spaces. You will need a large-scale map of the area, colored pencils, and a notebook.

Lichen on stones

Ants on wall

Bird's nest

Frog's eggs

1 Use the large-scale map to sketch or trace an outline map of your chosen area. Draw in the roads and buildings. Ask an adult to walk around the area with you.

2 Make notes or take photos of different ecosystems. There are often small ecosystems within larger ones. Look for living things interacting with nonliving things, such as insects on a wall.

3 Mark on the map the locations of all the ecosystems you have observed, using different patterns or symbols for each ecosystem. Draw the symbols with pencil first, then color them in.

4 Each ecosystem should be easy to recognize. A meadow, for example, could be shown by a tuft of grass. Design a key to explain the symbols and patterns you have used. Print names beside each one.

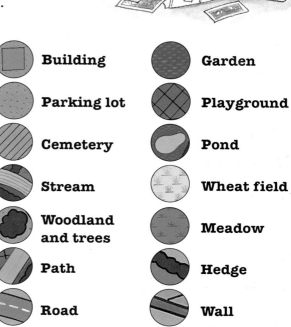

Litter

- Building
- Parking lot
- Cemetery
- Stream
- Woodland and trees
- Path
- Road
- Garden
- Playground
- Pond
- Wheat field
- Meadow
- Hedge
- Wall

5 Now add to your map any other details you have observed. Depending upon the season, you may have noticed a bird's nest or a fox's lair. Or you may have noticed parts of an ecosystem damaged by litter pollution.

LIVING AND NONLIVING

● An ecosystem is a jigsaw puzzle of living and nonliving parts. The Sun and weather play a part in every ecosystem. Each part is vital. They are interdependent— if one piece is lost, the whole ecosystem breaks down. Make a list of the living and nonliving parts of your ecosystems.

Ecosystem	Living parts	Nonliving parts
Pond	Frogs, dragonflies, water lilies, pondweed	Water, stones, air, sunshine

WHO EATS WHAT?

All living things in an ecosystem depend upon each other for food. They are linked together in a food web. In a healthy ecosystem, there must be a balance between the number of living things that exist there. This balance is called the food pyramid. Usually, there are far fewer carnivores (meat eaters) than herbivores (plant eaters). The carnivores keep the number of herbivores under control. Most natural ecosystems, on land and in water, get their energy from the Sun. The Sun's energy is passed through the food pyramid.

FOOD PYRAMID

4. Large carnivores eat herbivores and small carnivores. So they are both secondary and tertiary (third-level) consumers.

3. Small carnivores eat herbivores. They are secondary (second-level) consumers.

1. Plants are producers— they produce their own food using energy from the Sun.

2. Herbivores are primary (first-level) consumers. They eat green plants directly. They are prey to large and small carnivores.

FOOD WEB

Food webs show all the members of an ecosystem community and how they interact with each other. Make your own food web to show who eats what.

Person

Bird of prey

Rabbit

Sheep

Plants

Air

Sun's energy

1 Cut out pictures of living things found in a wood. Draw and cut out a picture of the Sun, water, and a cloud (for air). Glue your pictures onto folded strips of cardboard.

2 Stand the cards up. Use ribbon and tape to attach each animal to its food. Use red ribbon for carnivores and green ribbon for herbivores. Trace each ribbon with your finger to see how all the plants and animals are interlinked.

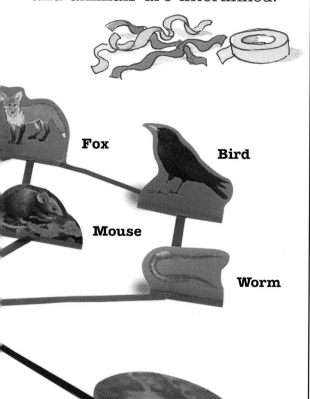

Fox

Bird

Mouse

Worm

Water

ENERGY FROM THE SUN

● Each chain of links in a food web, joining plants to herbivores and carnivores, is called a food chain. Most food chains start with the Sun.

● Chlorophyll, the green color in leaves, uses the Sun's energy to make food. Sunlight turns molecules of water and a gas called carbon dioxide into sugar inside the leaf. This process is called photosynthesis.

Sugar

● In this simple food chain, a cabbage makes food using sunshine. The Sun's energy passes to the caterpillar when it eats a cabbage leaf. A bird then eats the caterpillar. When the bird dies, decomposers —small creatures and plants such as insect larvae and fungi—break down its body into the soil. This enriches the soil, which plants then use to help them grow.

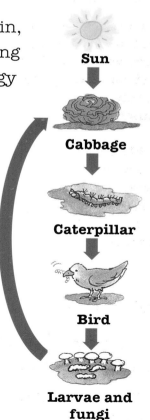

Sun

Cabbage

Caterpillar

Bird

Larvae and fungi

AN OAK TREE

An oak tree supports a small ecosystem. The tree is broad-leaved and deciduous, which means it loses its leaves in winter. The oak is a rich habitat for animals and birds, which find food and building materials on and around the tree. At ground level, there are worms, insects, leaf litter, dead wood, flowers, grasses, and fungi. From the ground beneath the tree to the canopy—the top of the tree—a variety of living things can be observed.

WHAT'S IN A TREE?

Make a seasonal diary for the ecosystem of an oak tree. You will need paper, string, twigs, an old umbrella, and colored pencils.

Spring

Date/time	Weather	
April 12th 11 A.M.		**Squirrel**—gray
April 15th 1 P.M.		**Worm castings**—lots on ground under tree
April 16th 4 P.M.		**Green woodpecker**—green body, red on head—making a drumming noise on tree trunk
April 18th 10 A.M.		**Wood ants**—running up tree trunk / **Primrose**—pale yellow flowers, 5 petals, short stems, thick, dark leaves

1 Hang the open umbrella from a lower branch on the tree. Shake the branch lightly. Describe or sketch any minibeasts that fall into your umbrella trap. Record your findings, then return the minibeasts to their habitat.

2 Ask an adult to help you press some twigs firmly into the ground around the tree. Use string to make a circle on the ground around the twigs. Write down, sketch, or photograph anything you see inside the circle, such as worm castings, old acorn shells, and leaves.

3 Look for small mammals and birds, such as crows, magpies, or even a sparrow hawk, in the tree. Are any birds nesting? If there is a hole in the trunk, there may be a woodpecker's nest. Listen for bird songs.

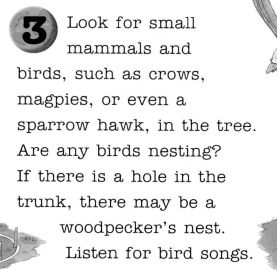

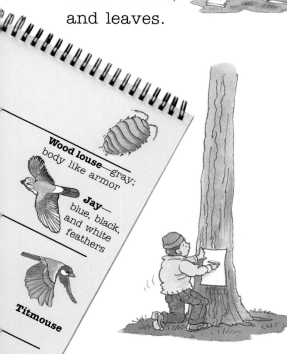

Wood louse—gray; body like armor

Jay— blue, black, and white feathers

Titmouse

4 Write headings, for time, date, and weather. Write in your observations and stick in sketches, photographs, and even bark rubbings. Add labels to build up a complete picture of an oak tree ecosystem.

ON AND UNDER OAKS

● As seasons change, the oak tree menu changes for the wildlife in and around it. In the fall, large birds and mammals eat acorns. In spring, jays and magpies eat eggs stolen from nests. Titmice eat caterpillars on leaves and buds.

● Nature recycles its waste. Under a tree, you will find decomposers that feed and grow on dead plants and animals, breaking them down into the soil (see below). Decomposed matter does not hold energy, but provides the soil with nutrients (goodness).

Fungi grow on dead logs and leaves.

Ants, beetles, and other small creatures eat droppings and fungi.

Bacteria break down anything that remains.

GLOBAL ECOSYSTEMS

The world is split into large ecosystems called biomes. Biomes are named after the main type of vegetation (plant life) that grows there. They are shaped by climate—how hot, cold, wet, or dry a place is. Tropical forests have lots of rain and sunshine. Deserts are hot and dry. The tundra (cold desert) is freezing. Mountaintops are also cold. Temperate regions have a warm, moist climate and are rarely very hot or very cold. Each place has its own food web, with wildlife that has adapted to the climate there.

Tundra
Coniferous forest
Temperate grasslands
Temperate forest
Mountains
Desert
Scrub
Savanna
Seasonal tropical forest
Tropical rainforest

Climate depends upon latitude (how far north or south of the equator a place is), and altitude (height above sea level).

Ice
Tundra
Coniferous forest
Temperate grasslands
Temperate forest
Scrub
Mountains
Desert
Savanna
Seasonal tropical forest
Tropical rainforest

Equator

Biomes of the world

ISLANDS
● Islands often have unique ecosystems. The Galapagos Islands, off the coast of Ecuador, are home to some of the world's rarest creatures, such as giant tortoises and sea lizards (right).

BIOME CARD GAME

To make this game, you will need thin cardboard, scissors, and colored pencils. Each set of cards shows a food chain in a different biome.

1 Cut out 30 pieces of cardboard. Copy the pictures on the cards shown here, until you have two sets of each food chain and six Sun cards. Number and label each set, as shown.

Sun (all sets) x 6

Temperate forest set

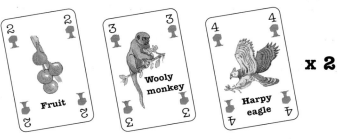
x 2

Tropical rainforest set

x 2

Tundra set

x 2

Desert set

x 2

2 Two or more can play. The aim is to collect four cards belonging to the same set. All sets must include a Sun card (1). Each player begins with four cards. Take turns to pick a card from the pile. Either keep that card or replace it at the bottom of the pile. The first person to collect a whole food chain is the winner.

ADDING MORE CARDS
● Find out about more food chains, in these or other biomes, and make cards for them. Make sure you always have a plant, a herbivore, and a carnivore. Make up a symbol for each new biome.

CONIFEROUS FORESTS

Coniferous trees have soft wood and needlelike leaves that stay green throughout the year. They grow best in cold climates and on mountainsides. In a coniferous forest, sunshine rarely reaches the forest floor, so ecosystems are not nearly as rich as in broad-leaved forests, because few plants grow with so little light. The diversity (variety) of wildlife is not as great, because there are fewer plants for animals and birds to eat. There are not many natural coniferous forests left today—most are now planted by foresters.

Dry

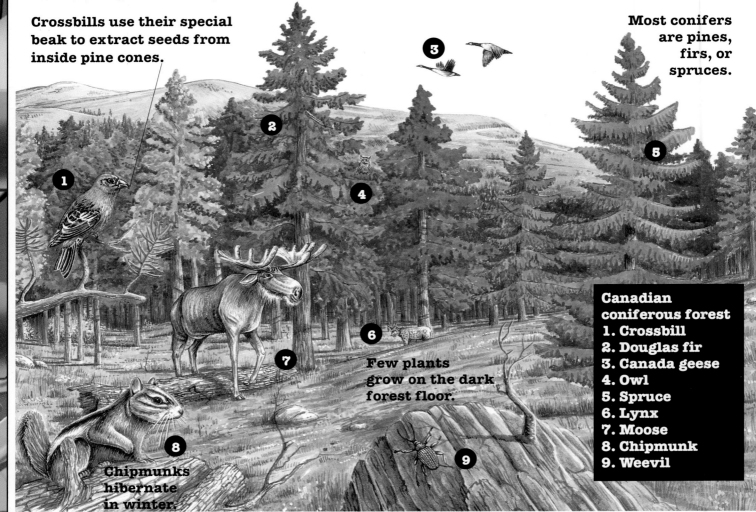

Crossbills use their special beak to extract seeds from inside pine cones.

Most conifers are pines, firs, or spruces.

Few plants grow on the dark forest floor.

Chipmunks hibernate in winter.

Canadian coniferous forest
1. Crossbill
2. Douglas fir
3. Canada geese
4. Owl
5. Spruce
6. Lynx
7. Moose
8. Chipmunk
9. Weevil

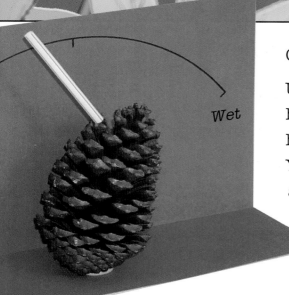

Wet

CONE GAUGE

Use a pine cone to make a hygrometer. This measures humidity—moisture in the air. You will need a pine cone, a pushpin, a plastic drinking straw, cardboard, modeling clay, and a pen.

1 Stick the pushpin into one of the middle scales of the cone. Push a straw over the end of the pushpin.

2 Fold the cardboard and draw a scale on it, as shown below. Position the cone on the cardboard using modeling clay. Place it outside, sheltered from rain. Wait and see which way the straw moves in moist air. Now label the scale "wet" at one end and "dry" at the other end.

WHAT'S HAPPENING

● Pine cones hold the seeds of conifers. They close when the air is moist and it is about to rain, to protect the seeds inside. The outside scales absorb the moisture in the air, swell up, and bend inward to close.

Seed

SUSTAINABLE FORESTRY

● In many parts of the world, the wildlife-rich natural vegetation has been cut down and replaced by coniferous forests. The conifers are then cut down to make paper and furniture. Now foresters practice sustainable forestry. This means they cut down only part of the coniferous forests at one time so that ecosystems can survive.

TROPICAL RAINFORESTS

Many of the world's plant and animal species live in tropical rainforests, where the climate is always warm and moist. The Amazon rainforest in South America is like a huge apartment building, with different species living at each level. At the bottom is the dark forest floor, then the herb layer, shrub layer, understory, canopy, and, at the top, the emergent layer. Hardwood trees grow tall and straight as they struggle to reach the sunlight. They are so tall that they have roots above the ground.

Emergent layer—the tallest trees push through the canopy to reach the Sun.

Understory—younger trees strive to reach the sunlight.

Herb layer—ferns and herbs grow. Tapirs and insects live here.

Canopy—treetops are bound together by creepers and climbing plants. Home to orchids, birds, monkeys, snakes, and lizards.

Shrub layer—young trees grow from seedlings. Woody plants with large leaves and colorful flowers grow here.

Forest floor—rotting leaf litter covers the poor soil. Few plants grow here, except along rivers, where some sunshine gets through.

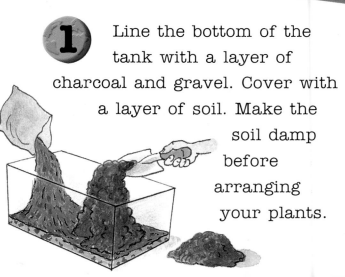

MINIRAINFOREST

To create a minirainforest, you will need a small fish tank with a lid (or use plastic wrap), soil, charcoal, gravel, and suitable plants, such as ferns, mosses, orchids, and African violets.

1 Line the bottom of the tank with a layer of charcoal and gravel. Cover with a layer of soil. Make the soil damp before arranging your plants.

2 Arrange the plants before planting. Do not put them too close together as they will need room to grow.

WHAT'S HAPPENING

● Rainforests play a big part in controlling the world's climate. Without trees, there would be less rainfall. Leaves transpire, which means they lose water through tiny holes. Transpiration helps make the air moist. The leaves on the plants in your tank will transpire and keep the air and soil moist.

● Thunderstorms are frequent in rainforests as the warm, moist air rises quickly and cools.

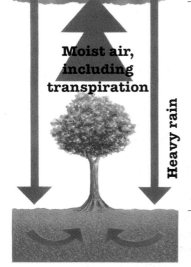

Fast-rising moist air condenses into droplets, which form high thunderclouds.

Cool air

Moist air, including transpiration

Warm air

Heavy rain

Soil is kept moist

EPIPHYTES

● Epiphytes are rainforest plants that grow on other plants. Some grow in the low, darker parts of the forest. Others, like orchids, like the sunshine of the canopy.

DEFORESTATION

● Half the world's rainforests have been destroyed. Some people cut down trees to farm the land for food. Others cut down trees to sell the lumber.

3 Place the lid (or plastic wrap) over the tank and put in a warm spot, but not in direct sunlight. Water every few weeks. The lid will keep the soil moist.

HOT DESERTS

Living things struggle to survive in hot, dry deserts. Many have learned some very strange habits, just to stay alive. The spadefoot toad, found in the Sonoran Desert of Arizona, hibernates underground for most of the year. When the annual midsummer rain approaches, it emerges to mate and lay its eggs in pools of rainwater. Within days, the eggs hatch and become tadpoles, then toads. Then the toads disappear underground again. Desert plants have to survive for long periods without rain. Many survive as seeds. Cacti have shallow roots, close to the surface, ready to catch any rain that falls.

PLANT A DESERT GARDEN

To create a desert garden, you will need a shallow clay bowl, sand and soil, pebbles or gravel, protective gloves, and some small cactus plants. Ask at your local plant nursery for advice on which cacti to buy.

1 Mix together the sand and soil. Fill the bowl three-quarters full with the soil mixture.

2 Put on protective gloves, then plant your cacti. After planting, cover the surface of the soil with pebbles or gravel.

DESERT ANIMALS AND PEOPLES

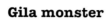
Gila monster

● Desert animals have had to adapt to hot, dry conditions. In North America, a poisonous lizard called the Gila monster stores fat in its thick tail. It can live on this fat for months without eating. Birds called roadrunners save energy by running instead of flying. Ground squirrels in the Kalahari Desert in southern Africa use their plumed tails as sunshades.

● For thousands of years, the only people living in the Great Australian Desert were Aboriginal nomads—people who regularly move from place to place. Now, most Australian Aborigines live in towns and cities. Bedouins have lived in the deserts of North Africa and Syria for centuries. A few still live as nomads, traveling from oasis to oasis.

Bedouins

HELPFUL HINTS

● Place your desert garden in a sunny position.

● Cacti have sharp spikes, so handle them with care. Use thick leather or suede gloves to protect your hands when handling cacti.

● Do not water your garden too often. Cacti need only a small amount of water. Too much water will cause the stems to rot and will leave a black mark.

COLD DESERTS

Cold deserts, called tundra, are places where the ground is frozen for much of the year. Alpine tundra is found at high altitudes, above the tree line. In the Arctic, there are no trees, only grasses, mosses, and lichens. Lichens are fungi that contain algae. They appear as crusty patches or shrubby growths on rocks. Shrubby lichens can only survive in clean air. They are an important part of tundra ecosystems, and are threatened by pollution, which can be carried a great distance by winds and water.

North of the tundra is the Arctic icecap.

Below the surface is permafrost, which is ground that is frozen all year round.

The tundra has rocky mounds, called pingoes, and long lakes.

Below the tundra is a belt of coniferous forest, called the taiga.

LOOKING FOR LICHENS

One way to check pollution in your area is to look for lichens. The nature and color of any lichens will indicate air quality. If you find only green algae, the air is probably heavily polluted.

1 Ask an adult to come with you to look at local lichens. Look on walls, stones, trees, and gravestones. Record the color and location of any lichens you see. Sketch their appearance. Check the scale opposite to help you identify the lichens.

2 Mark your lichen findings on the ecosystems map you made on page 82. Make up a key to show the type of lichen found. Write down the date on which you found them.

Polluted

GREEN ALGAE
Found in heavily polluted areas. Probably no lichens.

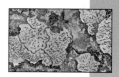

GRAY-GREEN CRUSTY LICHENS
Often found on gravestones. High-level air pollution.

ORANGE CRUSTY LICHENS
Also found on gravestones. Medium-level air pollution.

LEAFY LICHENS
Found on walls and trees. Low-level air pollution.

SHRUBBY LICHENS
Found on rocks and trees. Clean air.

Clean

Lichens can live for 4,000 years. They can survive all climatic conditions. There are 25,000 known species. They grow slowly, only half an inch a year.

SYMBIOSIS AND CAMOUFLAGE

● Symbiosis is a partnership between two living things, from which both benefit. The fungi and algae that make up lichens are symbiotic. The fungi absorb water and minerals, then the algae use these to turn

sunshine into food by photosynthesis (see page 85). Both the fungi and algae gain from living together.

● Camouflage is the ability of certain animals to blend in with their natural surroundings and so hide from predators. But predators also use camouflage to hide from their prey.

Arctic fox in summer

Arctic fox in winter

FRESHWATER ECOSYSTEMS

In ponds and lakes, where the water is still, plant life is rich. Rivers and streams have running water, so there is less plant life. Large predators like perch eat smaller fish. Too many predators in a pond destroy the ecosystem because the secondary consumers are all eaten up. Without secondary consumers to control numbers, the primary consumers increase and eat all the plant life. Without plant life, the pond ecosystem breaks down completely.

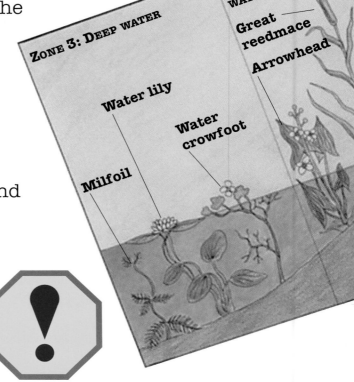

ZONE 3: DEEP WATER

ZONE 2: SHALLOW WATER OR SWAMP

Great reedmace

Arrowhead

Water lily

Water crowfoot

Milfoil

POND ZONES

Pond animals move around, but plants remain in one place. Make a pond chart, dividing it into zones according to the plants found there. Be careful near water. Always tell an adult what you are doing.

1 Make sketches and take notes about the plants in and around the pond. Look first at the bank, then at the shallow water, or swampy area around the edge, then at the deep water. Here, you will only be able to see the tops of the plants. Some plants live completely under the water.

Zone 1: Bankside

Meadow sweet

Marsh marigold

Great pond sedge

Water iris

2 Sketch a cross section of the pond and divide it into zones, as shown here. Zone 1 is the bankside, Zone 2 is the shallow water or swamp area, and Zone 3 is the deep water. Underwater plants, called submerged aquatics, go in the deep water zone. Fill in details about each plant. Use a field guide to help you identify any plants not shown here.

POND LIFE

● Birds that live and feed near fresh water have adapted special feet and beaks. The heron has a long, thin beak with which to catch fish or frogs. It has long legs so it can stand for a long time in deep water waiting for prey.

Flamingo

Heron

Avocet

● Everything in a pond food web depends on plant life, even if you cannot see any plants. Big fish eat small fish, which eat dragonfly larvae, which eat tiny creatures, which feed on microscopic plants.

Dragonfly

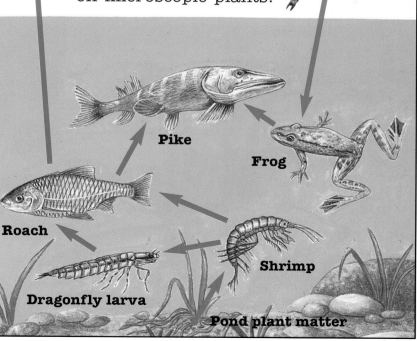

Pike

Frog

Roach

Shrimp

Dragonfly larva

Pond plant matter

ON THE SEASHORE

There are sandy, pebble, and rocky beaches. Each provides a different habitat, but all are affected by the same tidal movements. There are two high and two low tides every day. Very high tides, called spring tides, happen twice a month. Between high-water spring tide marks and low-water spring tide marks, there are five seashore zones. In these zones, plants and animals have adapted to produce a variety of ecosystems. Different seaweeds and shells are found in each zone.

BEACHCOMBER

Next time you go to a beach, carry out a beach ecosystem survey. Tell an adult where you are going and ask a friend to come with you. Always check the times of high tides. Carry out your study at low tide. Select a quiet stretch of beach to study.

Splash zone

Upper shore

High tide mark

Middle shore

Lower shore

1 Stretch a length of string from the top of the beach to the edge of the water. Hold each end in place with a pebble. Mark the string with a pen where you think each zone ends. The five zones are lower shore, middle shore, upper shore, high tide mark, and splash zone.

2 List the differences you notice between the zones. Collect shells, pebbles, and small pieces of seaweed and driftwood. Note carefully which zone you found them in. Record the date, time, and weather conditions.

JETSAM

● Storms at sea often carry jetsam (trash from ships) onto beaches. Ropes, bottles, and cans are found among seaweed and shells after bad weather. Containers holding dangerous chemicals have been found on beaches. They can gradually alter ecosystems.

SAND DUNES

● Grasses have long roots that hold the sand down in ridges. This prevents the sand from blowing away. Grasses are often planted in sand dunes to stop the sand from blowing any farther.

ROCK POOLS

● Rock pools are left behind when the tide goes out. Plants and animals that live in rock pools cannot survive out of water. In rock pools you may find sea anemones, crabs, sea urchins, starfish, seaweeds, and shrimp. Small fish are also found in pools. Always replace rocks that you move.

3 Map the area of beach you have surveyed onto a sheet of cardboard. Draw in the zones created by high- and low-water marks. Glue on and label everything you have collected.

Rock pool

SALTWATER ECOSYSTEMS

The ocean is the largest habitat on Earth. But sea animals depend upon plants for their food, just as land animals do. The most important marine plants, called phytoplankton, are so small that they can only be seen with a microscope. Phytoplankton are the primary producers in the food chains of the sea. They grow near the surface, where sunlight causes photosynthesis to happen. Microscopic animals called zooplankton then feed on phytoplankton, and larger animals eat the zooplankton.

Orca

Tern

Seal

Fish

Squid

OCEAN FOOD WEB

Phytoplankton are single-celled algae. If you get a chance, look at a sample of sea water under a microscope, and you will see the pretty patterns on phytoplankton.

Krill

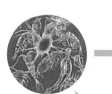

Zooplankton

Phytoplankton

SALTY FACTS

● A food web of the sea includes some of the smallest and largest living things in the world—the blue whale and krill. Krill are tiny shrimplike forms of zooplankton, found in the seas of the Antarctic. Amazingly, they are the only food the blue whale eats. The blue whale can be over 90 feet long. It strains the krill from the ocean through the baleen inside its mouth, which acts like a strainer.

Blue whale

Krill

1. Corals grow around a volcanic island.

2. The volcano erodes and a lagoon forms.

3. The volcano sinks completely. The reef remains, with small, sandy islands on top.

● In tropical seas, low islands called coral reefs are formed by tiny creatures called polyps. The jellylike polyps build up hard skeletons of calcium carbonate. When they die, the skeletons are left as coral. New polyps grow on top of the dead ones. Coral needs warmth and light, so it grows only near the ocean's surface.

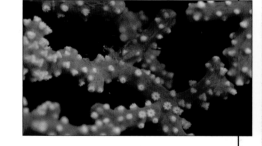

● Coastal mangrove swamp forests are types of tropical forest. Mangrove trees have adapted to survive in the salty water in mud estuaries of tropical rivers. They have special roots that keep the leaves above the water and allow the plant to obtain more oxygen. Mangroves are the habitat of many species, such as fiddler crabs, and are breeding grounds for reef fish.

WILDLIFE GARDEN

As your contribution toward preserving healthy ecosystems, you could make a wildlife garden. Even if you do not have your own garden, you can encourage wildlife by cultivating plants in a windowbox or on a balcony. Plant flowers with strong colors and scents that will attract insects such as bees and butterflies. Peacock butterflies like to lay their eggs beneath nettle leaves. These pages will give you some ideas on how to create a wildlife garden.

A SPACE FOR WILDLIFE

Diversity is the key to a successful wildlife garden. Diversity means providing many different habitats—shady areas, sunny spots, and open spaces. This will attract many creatures. You could make a habitat pile, from logs, to attract insects. Make a bird table so birds can feed safely. You could even build a pond.

HELPFUL HINTS

● Choose the east- or west-facing side of a tree trunk for a birdhouse. A south-facing nest may harm fledglings because they will become too warm.

● A log pile will encourage minibeasts into your wildlife garden. It will also encourage small birds like wrens which feed on insects.

● Leave an area of garden with long grass—this will also encourage minibeasts.

BIRD FEEDER

Make environmentally friendly pine cone bird feeders. You need some long pine cones, a ball of string, a spoon, unsweetened peanut butter, birdseed, waxed paper, and a baking tray.

1 First, cut a length of string for each pine cone. Loop and tie the string to one end of each cone.

2 Use a spoon to smear peanut butter all over each pine cone. Make sure it covers every part of the cone. Press firmly into all the spaces.

3 Sprinkle birdseed onto the waxed paper on the baking tray. Roll the cones in the birdseed until they are all well covered. The birdseed will stick to the peanut butter. Shake off any loose seed.

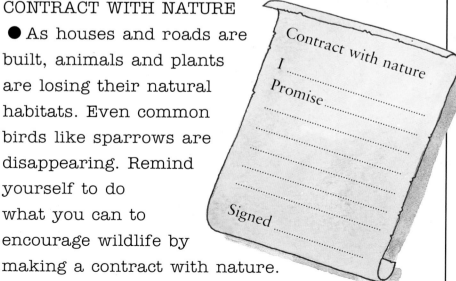

4 Birds like to feed where they are safe from predators like cats. Position your pine cone bird feeders away from shrubbery, trees, and fences. A tree stump or bird table in the center of an open space is a safe site.

CONTRACT WITH NATURE

● As houses and roads are built, animals and plants are losing their natural habitats. Even common birds like sparrows are disappearing. Remind yourself to do what you can to encourage wildlife by making a contract with nature.

Contract with nature

I ....

Promise ....

....

....

....

Signed ....

CHAPTER 5
People and Places

Some places in the world are very crowded, and there are others where hardly any people live. Find out why people live in certain places rather than others, and how the place we live affects our lifestyle. See how people build different kinds of houses in different parts of the world.

People change their surroundings when they chop down trees or build roads and houses. In this chapter, you will map your life journey so far, make your own windmill, and learn how to make paper!

CONTENTS

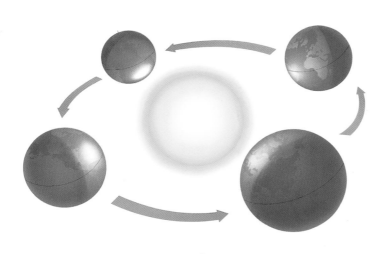

SETTLEMENTS

A settlement is a place where people live. It can be very small, with only a few houses, or as large as a city, where millions of people live. A city has lots of stores and offices and provides services, such as hospitals and schools, for its people. A long time ago, people built settlements close to rivers, because they provided water and were the best way to transport goods. New Orleans grew up at a good location on the Mississippi River.

Street map

x *My house*

Continent map

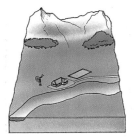

A house is built by a river for water and easy transportation.

Roads are built and a town forms as more people settle.

The town expands into a city, with services, factories, and many roads.

WHERE YOU LIVE

Make a "nest" of four maps, each on a different scale, to show the first four lines of your address.

Paola Zaghini
14 Appian Way
Rome
Italy
Europe
The Northern Hemisphere
The World
The Galaxy
The U

1 Use a large-scale map to find the street you live on.

2 Find the location of your village, town, or city in an atlas. Is there a river nearby? Now find your country. What shape is it? Does it have a coastline? Find the name of the continent in which you live.

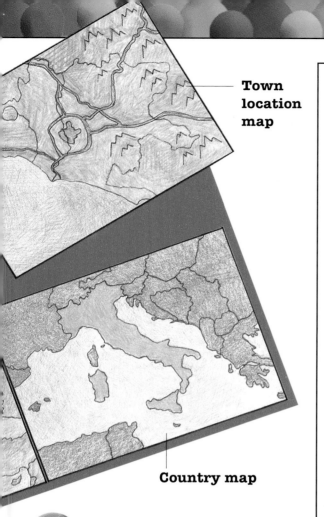

Town location map

Country map

3 Now draw four maps, as shown. Make sure you put in natural features, like rivers. Glue the maps onto cardboard and label them.

HELPFUL HINTS

● The scale on each map is different. A street map is large-scale; a continent map is small-scale. To get the scale right, trace from the atlas.

● Practice using scale by doing map "nests" for places you hear about in the news.

TYPES OF SETTLEMENT

● The area around a settlement is its location. A village is a rural location, which means it is surrounded by countryside. A town or city is an urban location—a built-up area, with many buildings and services.

CITY
Large urban location. Services include stores, offices, factories, places of worship, schools, hospitals, museums, theaters, restaurants, post offices, galleries, roads, and public transportation.

TOWN
Smaller than a city, but with similar services (in big towns). Small towns usually have one main shopping area.

VILLAGE
Up to 2,000 people. Services may include stores, a post office, a school, and public transportation.

HAMLET
Fewer than 50 people. Few services.

FARM or HOMESTEAD
One family. No services, except for electricity and telephone (in developed countries).

● Settlements built on the outskirts of cities are called suburbs. Suburbs sometimes stretch to join up with towns or villages nearby. Together, a city and its suburbs make a metropolitan area.

SHORT JOURNEYS

People make journeys every day. Each time you leave your house—to go to school, to a friend's house, or to the store—you are making a journey. There are different ways to travel a short distance—on foot or by bicycle, car, train, or bus. It usually takes longer to walk, but it is good exercise. People drive to supermarkets to shop. Parents often drive their children to school. Many people commute (travel to work each day) by car, bus, or train.

JOURNEY TIMES

Carry out a survey with a group of friends to find out how you all travel to school. Present your information on a chart. You will need cardboard, scissors, paper, glue, and colored pencils.

Brian
3 mi
20 mins

Tony
2 mi
15 mins

Lisa
2 $\frac{1}{2}$ mi
20 mins

Tasmin
$\frac{1}{4}$ mi
5 mins

Jin Soo
1 $\frac{1}{2}$ mi
15 mins

1 First, write out a list of questions to ask. Do you travel to school by car, bus, or train? Do you walk or bicycle? How far from school do you live? How long does your journey take? Record all of your friends' answers on a sheet of paper.

2 Cut out a strip of colored cardboard for each friend. Cut one end of each cardboard strip into an arrow shape.

PEDESTRIANS

● People who walk along sidewalks and footpaths are called pedestrians. In Britain, some children walk to school in a "walking bus." Parents lead the "bus" and collect children along the route.

● Children in some parts of the world have to walk many miles each day to get to school.

3 Draw a symbol of your school in the center of a large cardboard circle. Arrange the arrows around the school. Draw transportation symbols, as shown here. Glue the correct symbol onto each arrow. Write labels on small slips of paper to show how far each person travels and how long it takes.

Car

Bus

Bicycle

Walk

Anna
$1/_2$ mi
10 mins

Demi
$3/_4$ mi
10 mins

Alex
2 mi
6 mins

4 Now rearrange the arrows to show how each person travels home from school. Do they use the same forms of transportation as they used in the morning? Make new arrows, symbols, and labels for any changes.

SERVICES CHART

● Redo the chart to show the services you visit from home, such as stores and the library. Put your home at the center of the circle and arrange the arrows to show which form of transportation you use to get to each service. Write labels to show distances and journey times.

LONG JOURNEYS

In earlier times, large numbers of people moved from one region to another, seeking better living conditions and opportunities. But traveling was hard, and people moved short distances. Today, we live in a global community, in which many people can travel long distances quickly and easily. The result is that people from many different countries now live in cities like New York or London, yet keep their ties to family members in their countries of origin.

A MOVING STORY

Make a "family map" to show all the places that you and your family have links with. You need a large map of the world, a pencil, tracing paper, colored yarn, scissors, and pushpins.

Grandparents' generation (2 twists)

1 Do some research about your family tree. Ask questions and look in family albums. Where were you born? Where were your parents and grandparents born? If you have a stepfamily, include them in your research too.

2 Trace the part of the world map you need. It may be just one country if your family has always lived there. Color it and label the continents, countries, or towns. Mark your birthplace in pencil. Draw an arrow from there to the place you lived next, then to the place after that, and so on.

3 Cut lengths of yarn. Choose a different color for each generation of your family. Pin one end of your color of yarn to the place where you were born. Follow the arrows with the yarn, pinning it at each new place.

Parents' generation (1 twist)

4 To show the "life journey" taken by your parents and grandparents, twist different colors of yarn around your first strand. Add a twist for each generation. Place and pin the twists as you did for your own life journey. Write labels to show the dates your family moved from place to place.

MIGRATION

● People move for many different reasons, both within their own country and to other countries. Some move to live near family members who have already migrated.

● Some families move from the countryside to large cities to look for work. Most people in developed countries now live in urban areas.

● Some people escape the pollution and litter of cities to live in the countryside. Sometimes, they commute (travel every day) to work in the city.

● People who are forced to leave their own country, because they are living in danger, are called refugees. They seek refuge (a place to feel safe) in other countries. There are many thousands of refugees in the world today. Some escape from war or cruelty, and others flee from natural disasters, such as earthquakes or floods.

WORLD WEATHER

Climate—the usual pattern of weather in a place—affects the way people live. Climate depends mainly on latitude, which is how far north or south of the equator a place is (see below). Countries in tropical latitudes, close to the equator, have a hot, wet climate. Countries in temperate latitudes (between the tropics and the poles) have a mild climate. Altitude, which means height above sea level, also affects climate. Places at high altitudes are always cool, no matter where in the world they are.

LATITUDE AND LONGITUDE

● Numbered lines on maps and globes show latitude (horizontal lines) and longitude (vertical lines). Latitude is measured north or south of the equator, the zero degree (0°) line of latitude. The tropics lie between 0° and 23°N and 23°S. Temperate regions lie between the tropics and 60°N and 60°S. Longitude is measured in degrees east or west of the prime meridian, which runs through London, England.

Prime meridian
60°N
Temperate region
23°N
Tropics
Equator, 0°

CHART IT

Make a chart to show the climate in cities in different parts of the world. You will need an atlas, tracing paper, pencils, a ruler, scissors, and glue.

Aswan
24°N, 32°E
Aswan is in Egypt, on the bank of the Nile River. The climate is very hot and dry—it hardly ever rains there. July is the hottest month.

Bogota
4°N, 74°W

1 Look in the atlas index to find the country and continent in which each city is located. Trace country maps from the atlas and mark the location of each city you have chosen. Glue the maps onto your chart. Find the latitude and longitude for each city from the numbers on the atlas map grids.

Write labels about each place. Does it get a lot of rain? Which is the hottest month?

Temperature °F
110
90
70
50
30
10
-10

J F M A M J J A S O N D

Rainfall = virtually none

Bogota is in Colombia. It is very high, so it never gets very hot.

Temperature °F
90
70
50
30
10
-10

Rainfall, inches
20
16
12
8
4
0

J F M A M J J A S O N D

Manila is in the Philippines in Southeast Asia. It rains a lot and is hot most of the year. The climate is very humid.

Temperature °F
90
70
50
30
10
-10

Rainfall, inches
20
16
12
8
4
0

J F M A M J J A S O N D

Manila
14°N, 121°E

Latitude and longitude

2 Find monthly temperature and rainfall averages from the atlas. Put these in graphs, then glue the graphs on your chart. If you cannot find monthly rainfall, write in average yearly rainfall.

SEASONS

● Places in temperate regions have four seasons a year. Seasons happen because the Earth tilts on its axis as it circles the Sun. As one hemisphere (half of the Earth) leans toward the Sun, it has summer, while the other hemisphere leans away, and has winter. The Earth takes a full year to circle the Sun. The Sun shines almost directly over the equator all year, so it is always hot there.

Summer in the southern hemisphere

Winter in the northern hemisphere

Sun

Equator

Summer in the northern hemisphere

Winter in the southern hemisphere

● In tropical places, there are only two seasons each year, a wet season and a dry season. Floods often occur in the wet season. In rural parts of developing countries, this makes travel hard.

HOMES

Climate and location—whether a place is urban or rural—determine what kinds of home people build. In places with a cold climate, houses often have basements and double-glazed windows. In hot countries, homes must provide shade from the Sun. In areas with high rainfall, roofs must be sloped to let water run off easily. Urban locations in every climate usually have apartment houses, where many people can live in a small area.

TEMPERATE CLIMATE HOMES
Brick, stone, or wood, with big windows to let in light. Sloping roofs let rain run off easily.

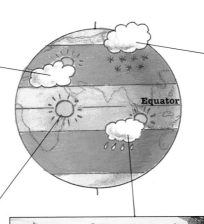

Equator

COLD CLIMATE HOMES
Sloping, ridged roofs with an overhang to protect balconies and people below from sliding snow. Often wooden walls.

HOT, DRY CLIMATE HOMES
Often rectangular, with a flat roof. Small windows and thick walls keep out the Sun.

HOT, WET CLIMATE HOMES
Often wooden walls, raised on platforms to allow cool air to circulate. Roofs often made from corrugated iron.

PLAY THE HOUSE GAME
Learn about climates and homes by making this card game for two players. You will need cardboard and colored pencils.

Temperate climate set

Cold climate set

1 First, copy and cut out two of each card shown here, so that you have 32 cards altogether. Each set represents one climate. Three cards show house types and one is the matching climate card.

2 Deal four cards each. Lay the remaining cards face down in a pile. The first player picks up the top card then throws a card away. Lay the unwanted cards face up in a pile. The next player can pick up the top card from either pile. The winner is the first to collect one full set.

Hot, wet climate set

Hot, dry climate set

SHANTY TOWNS

● In developing countries, many very poor people live in shanty towns on the outskirts of large cities. Most have moved near the city to find work. They live in makeshift shanties built of cardboard, corrugated metal, or plywood. The shanty towns have no running water or electricity.

A CROWDED WORLD

As population increases and more people need homes, many parts of the world are becoming overcrowded. A quarter of the world's population now lives in cities and the cities are gradually spreading into vast metropolitan areas. Some cities and countries are more crowded than others. France, for example, has the same population as Britain, but because France is bigger, it is less crowded. We say its population density is lower than Britain's. Population density is the average number of people per square kilometer (km^2) of land.

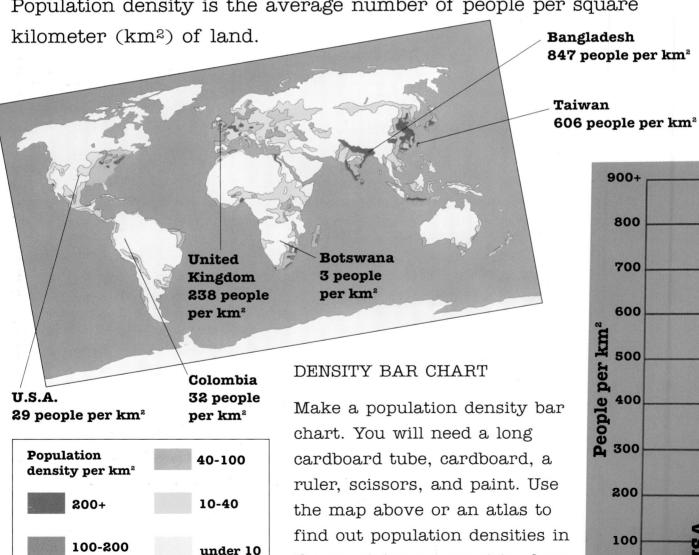

Bangladesh
847 people per km^2

Taiwan
606 people per km^2

United Kingdom 238 people per km^2

Botswana 3 people per km^2

U.S.A. 29 people per km^2

Colombia 32 people per km^2

Population density per km^2	
200+	40-100
100-200	10-40
	under 10

DENSITY BAR CHART

Make a population density bar chart. You will need a long cardboard tube, cardboard, a ruler, scissors, and paint. Use the map above or an atlas to find out population densities in the countries you want to show.

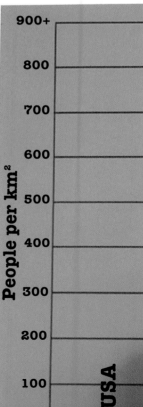

People per km^2

900+
800
700
600
500
400
300
200
100

USA

1 Choose a scale for your "bars," such as 5 cm (2 in) = 100 people per km². Measure and cut lengths of cardboard roll for each country. Paint and label each "bar."

2 Draw and label grid lines across the cardboard, starting about 20 cm (8 in) from the bottom. Fold the bottom to make a base. Glue the "bars" in place.

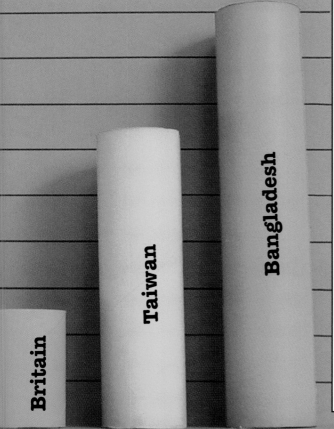

Britain

Taiwan

Bangladesh

POPULATION GROWTH

● The population of the world has greatly increased over the last 50 years. In 1999, the United Nations declared that the world's six billionth baby had been born in Bosnia.

10 million	200 million	420 million	1.2 billion	2.5 billion	6 billion	11 billion
100,000 years ago	2,000 years ago	500 years ago	1850	1950	2000	2050 (estimated)

● As population has grown, people have cleared more and more of the world's forests. Some are cut down to harvest the wood, some to make room to grow crops, and some to provide land for building houses and roads.

6,000 years ago   **2,000 years ago**   **Today**

Land   Forest   Forest   Land

● Population density can also be measured in people per square mile. If you know population per square kilometer, multiply that number by 2.59 to find the population per square mile.

RAW MATERIALS

Everything we use and everything around us is made from material of some kind. Materials that are changed or treated to be made into something else are called raw materials. One important raw material is cotton. The cotton plants need to be picked, cleaned, and processed before being made into fabric for clothes. Finished products, like cotton shirts, are called manufactured goods.

Limestone   **Iron ore**   **Coke**

Furnace

Iron

Iron ore is a mineral that is dug from the ground. It is heated in huge furnaces with coke and limestone. The iron separates as a very hot liquid and is poured into molds, where it cools and hardens.

ANIMAL, VEGETABLE, OR MINERAL?

Play this game to learn what different objects are made from. You will need small pictures of objects made from various materials, glue, and cardboard.

1 Draw or cut out pictures of objects from magazines. Glue each picture onto cardboard. Think about the raw materials used to make each one. A leather bag is made from animal hide (skin), so it is grouped as "animal." A book is made from wood pulp, so it is grouped as "vegetable." An iron railing is made from iron ore (see left), so it is classed as "mineral."

2 Write "animal," "vegetable," or "mineral" on the back of each object card. Use these pictures (right) to help you. Anything made from a plant is vegetable. Now quiz your friends. Hold up each card and ask, "Animal, vegetable, or mineral?" The player who gives the right answer keeps the card. The winner is the player with most cards.

String—vegetable (sisal or cotton)

Fork—mineral (metal)

Scarf—animal (wool)

Apple—vegetable (apple tree)

Glass—mineral (sand)

Cotton— vegetable (cotton plant)

Pencil—vegetable and mineral (wood and graphite)

Soap—animal or vegetable (animal or vegetable fat)

Plastic spoon— mineral (oil)

Leather shoes— animal (animal hide)

BRICKS
● Most bricks are made of clay and sand. These raw materials are ground together, then mixed with water and molded into

brick shapes. When the bricks have dried, they are fired in a very hot oven called a kiln to make them hard. The ancient Romans used triangular bricks, but most modern bricks are rectangular.
● To build walls, the finished bricks are laid in layers and stuck together with a cement mixture called mortar.

JOBS AND RESOURCES

People need to work to earn money to pay for food, clothing, and homes. A long time ago, most people worked on the land directly, as hunters or farmers. Then people began to work in manufacturing industries, using the Earth's natural resources—raw materials like wood—to turn into manufactured goods, such as paper. More people were then needed to work selling the manufactured goods. Today, few people work on the land in developed countries. Most work in offices and stores, or in jobs working with people, such as teaching.

PAPER-MAKING

Paper-making uses up one of the Earth's valuable natural resources —trees. The trees are cut down and the wood is turned into pulp, which is made into paper. You can save paper, and trees, by recycling old newspapers to make your own cards and paper.

Paper is rolled into huge sheets, then sold to printers to print newspapers and books.

1 You will need old newspapers, wire mesh, a dishpan, absorbent cloths, a blender, a bucket, thick paper (which you can keep and use again), and water. Tear the newspaper into pieces.

2 Put the pieces in a bucket and cover with water. Soak overnight. Ask an adult to put small amounts of the pulp into the blender and liquefy.

3 Decide on the size of your paper and ask an adult to cut the wire mesh to that size. Pour the liquefied pulp into the dishpan and add water. Stir the mixture. Slide the wire mesh into the mixture.

HIGH-TECH INDUSTRIES
● All over the world, industry is changing rapidly. Many people in India, for example, now work in high-tech industries, such as making computer parts. Many jobs that used to be done using pencil and paper, such as designing buildings, are now done on computers.

4 Lay a cloth flat on some thick paper. Lift the mesh out of the mixture and lay it on the cloth, pulp side down. Press down on the mesh, then lift it, leaving the layer of pulp on the cloth. Place another cloth, then more thick paper on top of the pulp and press. Repeat these layers, as shown.

Thick paper

Cloths

Thick paper

Cloths

Thick paper

Remember to keep all the thick paper to use again!

Add colored paper or flowers to the pulp for decoration.

5 Lay some heavy books on top of the last sheet of thick paper. Leave for a few days, then remove the layers. Place your sheets of paper on newspaper to dry. Use your recycled paper to make cards or writing paper.

ENERGY

Most of the energy we use in factories, homes, and cars is created from burning fossil fuels—oil, coal, and natural gas. Fossil fuels cause air pollution when they burn. They give off a gas called carbon dioxide, which gradually builds up in the Earth's atmosphere. Fossil fuels are also nonrenewable, which means they will not last forever. People are looking for other ways to make energy from sources that will not run out, such as the wind, light from the Sun, and running or falling water.

Burning fossil fuels (oil, coal, and gas) releases carbon dioxide gas.

Carbon dioxide builds up in the atmosphere.

Burning fossil fuels

Too much carbon dioxide in the atmosphere traps too much heat from the Sun. The Earth gets too warm, making ice melt and sea levels rise. This is called the greenhouse effect.

WIND POWER

Harness the power of the wind with a windmill. You will need thin paper, a length of dowel, a straight pin, a small bead, scissors, and a ruler.

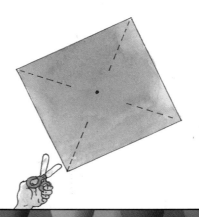

1 Cut out a square from the paper. Mark the center. Draw lines from each corner, almost to the center, as shown here. Cut along the lines.

2 Fold each corner into the center, as shown. Fix in place with a pin. Slide the bead onto the pin, behind the windmill.

3 Push the pin into the dowel, with the bead between the windmill and the dowel. Make sure the point of the pin does not stick out. Now stand in the wind and watch your windmill spin around as it captures the energy of the wind.

SOLAR POWER

● Solar energy comes directly from the Sun. Solar power stations (below) or solar panels attached to homes can capture energy from the Sun to provide heat and hot water. In hot deserts it is easy to catch the Sun's energy. It is more difficult in temperate countries that have lots of cloud and rain.

Solar panels

WIND POWER

● Wind turbines are set up in exposed places. The blades may spin through an area more than 200 feet across. The wind turns the turbine blades just as it spins your windmill. The turbines are connected to generators, which produce electricity. Wind energy is renewable and clean, but some say the turbines spoil the scenery.

COUNTRY PROFILE—KENYA

A country is a specific area of land, defined by humans, that is controlled by a single government. There are about 200 countries in the world.

Studying a country helps you see how different parts of geography fit together—how places and people affect each other. Kenya is a country in the continent of Africa. Its capital city is Nairobi. The zero degree (0°) line of latitude runs through Kenya, which means it is right on the equator, the hottest part of the world.

Kenyans mostly speak Kiswahili, but English is also spoken.

Kenya is close to Uganda, Ethiopia, and Tanzania.

PROJECT KENYA

Make a travel poster about Kenya and its people. You will need colored pencils, an atlas, and a large sheet of paper. First, look at a globe or an atlas to locate Africa.

North of the equator, Kenya is hot and has very little rain. South of the equator, there are 3 climatic regions: the humid coast, the temperate highlands, and the tropical region of Lake Victoria.

Coffee, tea, and sisal grow well in the tropical climate.

1 Write a list of the things that you need to find out about the country. What kind of climate does Kenya have? Does it have seasons? Are there any mountains? How high are they? Is there a coastline? Use the atlas, go to the library, or use the internet to find the information you need.

The rainy seasons are: October— December and April— June.

Mount Kenya is part of a chain of volcanic ridges.

TOURISM

● Tourism is one of Kenya's biggest industries. Hundreds of thousands of people visit every year and tourist activities provide jobs for thousands of local people. Many people come to visit the beautiful coastline, but most come to go on safari in one of the country's many national parks, such as Amboseli and the Masai Mara Game Reserve. The national parks are home to wild animals, such as lions, zebras, and elephants.

Kenyan national flag

The Kenyan flag is black, red, and green, with a shield and crossed spears logo in the center.

People eat *ugali*, a porridge made from cornmeal and water. They also eat *irio*, made from mashed corn, potatoes, beans, and peas.

In cities, Kenyans live in modern houses or apartments with plumbing and electricity. Farmhouses may be built from logs, branches, and mud. In Nairobi, houses are built from bricks.

2 There are many different tribal groups in Kenya, but most people are Kikuyu. Do some research to find out more about the Kenyan people. What languages do they speak? What kinds of houses do they live in? What are the main industries? What crops are grown? What do people eat? On your large sheet of paper, draw pictures and write labels for all the things you have found out about Kenya and its people.

LANDMARKS

Tourists visit landmarks all over the world. Some are specially built by humans, as monuments to a great event or person. The Taj Mahal in India was built by Shah Jehan in the seventeenth century as a tomb for his wife. Others are historic buildings or structures—such as Tower Bridge in London—which are famous for their design or for something that happened there in the past. Many landmarks are natural wonders, like waterfalls or mountains. Postcards often show landmarks.

Uluru, or Ayer's Rock, Australia

Taj Mahal, Agra, India

Tower Bridge, London, England

WHERE AM I?

Learn about landmarks in this game. You will need small pictures of different landmarks, cardboard, scissors, glue, and an atlas.

1 Collect postcards or cut out pictures from old magazines. Glue them onto pieces of cardboard.

2 Look in the atlas to find the location of every landmark. On the back of each card, write a few clues about the landmark, such as the capital of the country it is in.

3 Two or more players can play. One person is the tourist and holds up each picture in turn, asking "Where am I?" Players must guess the name of the country or city from the picture. Give clues if nobody gets it on the first try. Whoever gets the answer keeps the card. The winner is the player who collects the most cards.

CHANGING NAMES

● Names are like labels. But names on maps are often changed. Landmarks, streets, towns, and sometimes whole countries are given new names. Zaire, a country in Africa, was renamed the Democratic Republic of Congo. Czechoslovakia, in Eastern Europe, divided into two countries, the Czech Republic and Slovakia. The city of Constantinople is now Istanbul and Bombay is Mumbai.

● Settlements in different places often have the same name. There is a city called Birmingham in England and another one in Alabama, U.S.A. There is a Boston, England and a Boston, Massachusetts, U.S.A. Names can be clues to the past. Many people who

migrated and settled in other countries named their new homes with familiar names from their home countries.

CHAPTER 6

Food and Farming

Once, people had to hunt for food. Then they learned how to collect and grow grass seed and to herd animals, and farming had begun.

Now, the population of the world is growing fast, so more and more food is needed. Some farmers are changing their methods so that they can produce more crops. Learning about where food comes from will help you understand the importance of farming all over the world. In this chapter you will construct your own terraced slope, play "farminoes," and do an experiment to see how bananas help each other to ripen.

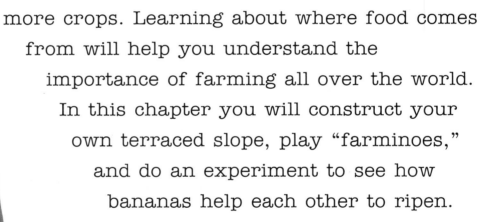

CONTENTS

POPULATION AND FOOD

In 1999, the population of the world reached 6 billion. Every person needs food to survive, so food supply has to increase as the number of people increases. The supply of food depends mainly on farmers. However, only certain parts of the Earth's surface are suitable for farming. Countries with the most people to feed—in parts of Africa, South America, and Asia—are also among the poorest areas of the world. Here, many farmers can produce only enough food for their own families.

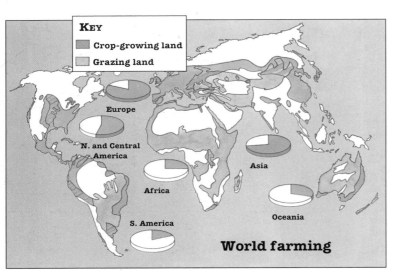

KEY
- Crop-growing land
- Grazing land

Europe

N. and Central America

Asia

Africa

S. America

Oceania

World farming

This map and the pie charts show roughly how much land in each continent is used for productive crop farming. Grassland areas are used for grazing livestock. The white areas are not used or are not suitable for farming.

UPS AND DOWNS OF FARMING

Farmers need good weather and rich soil or their crops will fail. Crops are also destroyed by disease and natural disasters. Make a game to show the ups and downs of farming.

1 Measure and rule a large grid of 10 x 10 squares on cardboard. Number the squares from 1 to 100, starting at the bottom left. Draw and color chutes and ladders onto the board, as shown on page 133.

2 Now use the key to help you design and draw symbols showing farming "ups"—things that help a food crop—and "downs"—things that destroy a food crop. Draw a "down" symbol at the top of each chute, and an "up" symbol at the bottom of each ladder.

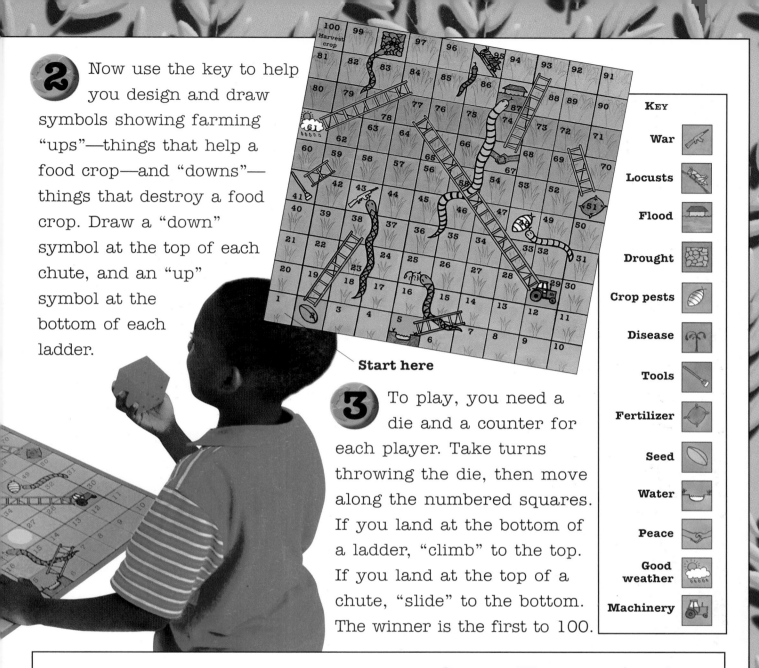

Start here

3 To play, you need a die and a counter for each player. Take turns throwing the die, then move along the numbered squares. If you land at the bottom of a ladder, "climb" to the top. If you land at the top of a chute, "slide" to the bottom. The winner is the first to 100.

KEY

War	
Locusts	
Flood	
Drought	
Crop pests	
Disease	
Tools	
Fertilizer	
Seed	
Water	
Peace	
Good weather	
Machinery	

STAPLE DIETS

● The food crop that grows best and is eaten most in any one country is called its staple diet. Most staple diets are cereal crops, like wheat. In developed countries, where food is plentiful, some people eat a staple diet of fast food, such as burgers.

Wheat, grown in temperate regions, is used to make bread and pasta.

Rice is the staple diet in many developing countries.

Maize, or corn, is the staple diet in parts of Africa and S. America. In the U.S., it is used mainly to feed livestock.

ALL YEAR ROUND

All farmers must prepare the soil, fertilize, plow, sow seed, nurture (look after), and harvest their crops. When these tasks are done depends upon climate and weather. In temperate climates, which are neither too hot nor too cold, farmers rely on the right kind of weather for each season. In spring, when seeds are sown, they hope for sunshine and showers. At harvest time, in late summer, they hope for dry weather with lots of sunshine. Farmers in the developed world use machinery to plant and harvest in large fields.

Plowing

A plow is a farm tool that turns over and breaks up the soil before seed is planted in the spring. Modern plows, such as the moldboard (left), are pulled by a tractor. They have metal blades that cut into the soil.

Sowing

In many developing countries, seed is still sown by hand. In developed countries, farmers use mechanical planters, or seed drills, pulled by tractors.

Growing and harvesting

Crops need rich soil, sunshine, and moisture to grow well. When they are ripe, the crops can be harvested quickly by combine harvesters. These machines combine the cutting and threshing (sorting grain from straw).

Grain

Threshing drum

Driver's cabin

Wheat

Straw

CLOUD-WATCHER

Clouds are made up of tiny water droplets. Rain falls when the droplets become too big. Farmers use clouds to forecast the weather. Make a chart to record the daily weather where you are.

1 Record the clouds each day for a week. What do they look like? Is any rain falling from them? Is the rain a drizzle or a downpour?

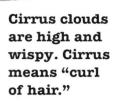

Cirrus clouds are high and wispy. Cirrus means "curl of hair."

Stratus clouds form a low, gray blanket. Stratus means "layer."

Cumulus clouds are either small and fluffy, or they tower into tall, billowing storm clouds. Cumulus means "heap."

2 Note the temperature each day. Place a thermometer outdoors, out of direct sunlight. Always take your readings at the same time each day.

Weather chart		
Date	**Temp.**	**Cloud & rain**
March 5th	50°F	rain all day
March 6th	48°F	drizzle
March 7th	51°F	no rain
March 8th	50°F	heavy rain
March 9th	55°F	clear sky, no rain
March 10th	53°F	no rain
March 11th	55°F	no rain

HELPFUL HINTS

● How many sayings about weather do you know? Keep a record to see if the ones you know are true or not.

SOIL

● When wind and rain erode (wear away) rock, they break it down into rock particles. These particles mix with humus to form soil. Humus is the decomposed (rotted) bodies of dead plants and animals. It binds the soil particles together and holds moisture.

Humus is found in topsoil and is rich in nutrients (goodness). Crops need nutrients to grow. Minibeasts like worms live here.

Subsoil contains more rock particles than humus. In rich soil, rainwater and roots should be able to reach into the subsoil.

Broken rocks lie between the subsoil and the bedrock. Groundwater can only seep as far as the bedrock. Very few roots reach here.

PRODUCING FOOD

The kind of farming practiced in temperate regions depends upon soil type and the condition of the land. Arable farming (the growing of crops) is done on low-lying land where the soil is rich. Sheep farming is done in hilly regions. Dairy farming is done on low-lying, rich grassland. Raising animals for food is called livestock farming. Poultry farmers raise birds, like chickens, for food. Mixed farming combines growing crops and raising animals. Truck farmers grow fruits and vegetables for sale in nearby cities.

FARMINOES

Learn about farms by playing "farminoes." You will need paper, cardboard, glue, scissors, and colored pencils.

1 Draw 28 domino shapes onto paper, then copy the farminoes shown below.

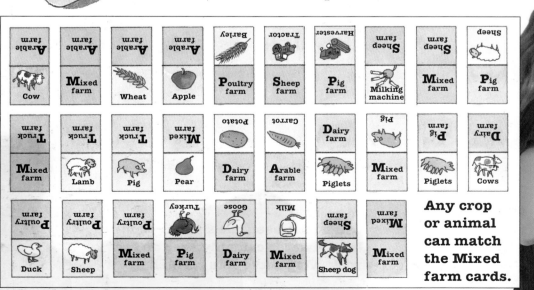

Arable farm	**A**rable farm	**A**rable farm	**A**rable farm	Barley	Tractor	Harvester	**S**heep farm	**S**heep farm	Sheep
Cow	**M**ixed farm	Wheat	Apple	**P**oultry farm	**S**heep farm	**P**ig farm	Milking machine	**M**ixed farm	**P**ig farm
Truck farm	**T**ruck farm	**T**ruck farm	**M**ixed farm	Potato	Carrot	**D**airy farm	Pig	**P**ig farm	**D**airy farm
Mixed farm	Lamb	Pig	Pear	**D**airy farm	**A**rable farm	Piglets	**M**ixed farm	Piglets	Cows
Poultry farm	**P**oultry farm	**P**oultry farm	Turkey	Goose	Milk	**S**heep farm	**M**ixed farm		
Duck	Sheep	**M**ixed farm	**P**ig farm	**D**airy farm	**M**ixed farm	Sheep dog	**M**ixed farm		

Any crop or animal can match the Mixed farm cards.

136

2 Ask an adult to help you glue your farminoes onto cardboard, then cut them out.

3 Divide the farminoes equally. Up to four people can play. The first player puts down a farmino, picture side up. The next player must match the crop or animal with the farm type, or the farm type with the crop or animal, as shown here. Take turns matching farminoes. If you cannot play, miss a turn. The winner is the first to have no farminoes left.

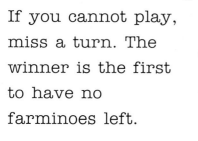

FACTORY FARMING
● On factory farms, egg-laying hens live side by side in cages with little room to move. Each hen lays more than 200 eggs a year, but many hens become sick and anxious. Some people prefer to buy free-range eggs, which are laid by hens that have more space to move around.

FOOD MOUNTAINS
● In developed countries, many farmers produce more food than they can sell, due to modern machines and intensive farming methods. The surplus (leftover) food is stored in huge "mountains." In developing countries, farmers cannot produce enough food. Many can only grow enough for their own families, so some people starve. Sometimes, the surplus food is used to help emergency food aid programs in areas where people are starving.

FARM TO TABLE

Farmers work directly with the earth, and are called primary producers. Many farm products, such as eggs, livestock, grains, and vegetables are processed by secondary producers to make other useful things. The products that come from corn (maize) include breakfast cereals and corn syrup, which is used to sweeten soft drinks. Wheat kernels are ground to a fine powder called flour, which is used to make bread. Fruits can be made into juices.

Wheat kernel

- Husk
- Bran
- Germ

White flour is made from the soft insides of the kernel.

1 Cut out 20 cards from the cardboard. Copy the pictures on the key opposite onto a sheet of paper. Cut each picture out and glue it onto one of your cards. Write the name of each crop or product on the card, as shown. Place the cards upside down in a pile.

FARMING PAIRS

Pair up farm crops and farm animals with the products made from them. You will need cardboard, paper, scissors, glue, and colored pencils.

2 Two can play. Deal five cards each. Take turns picking a card from the pile. If you can make a pair, lay it in front of you. The first to collect five matching pairs is the winner.

KEY

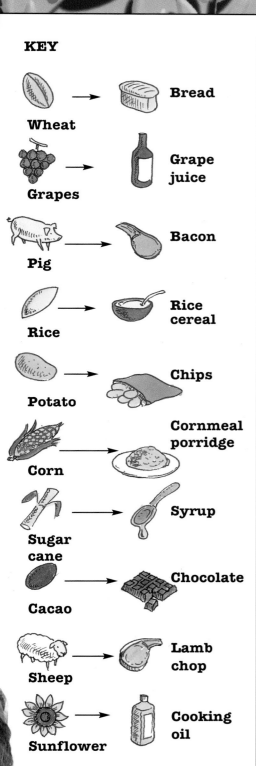

Wheat → Bread

Grapes → Grape juice

Pig → Bacon

Rice → Rice cereal

Potato → Chips

Corn → Cornmeal porridge

Sugar cane → Syrup

Cacao → Chocolate

Sheep → Lamb chop

Sunflower → Cooking oil

You can add more cards to the game by drawing other farm products and the things they are made into.

CATTLE

● Cattle are herbivores, which means they eat plants. They can graze over a large area, finding enough to eat even on poor grazing land. Products that come from cows include leather, milk, beef, and beef fat.

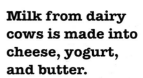

Cow hide is turned into leather for bags, jackets, and shoes.

Beef cattle are often sent to feed lots, where they can be fattened quickly before being butchered. They are fed concentrated food for quick growth.

Milk from dairy cows is made into cheese, yogurt, and butter.

Beef fat is used in cooking and is added to processed foods.

● Livestock can suffer from various diseases. In parts of Africa, the tsetse fly carries a parasite that feeds on the blood of cattle. BSE, or "mad cow disease," spread through several European countries in the 1990s. Thousands of cows were slaughtered (killed), and some people who ate infected meat died. Foot-and-mouth is a highly infectious disease that affects livestock, but is not dangerous to humans. In 1967 and 2001, there were outbreaks in Europe. Thousands of sheep and cattle were slaughtered and burned.

SUSTAINABLE FARMING

Farmers must be able to produce crops year after year. To do this, the soil must remain healthy and fertile. This is called sustainable farming. Modern farming methods and machinery have greatly increased the world's food supply, necessary to feed the growing population. Chemical pesticides and fertilizers are used to produce as many crops as possible. Farmers must make sure that their methods are sustainable—that the crops they plant and chemicals they

Pesticide

use do not destroy the goodness in the soil. Some prefer organic farming—using natural fertilizers.

MINIBEAST DETECTIVE

Minibeasts play a large role in keeping soil healthy. To see them, you need some soil, a large sieve, a fine sieve, a large jar, a magnifying glass, paper towels, and an adjustable lamp.

1 First, remove any sticks and stones from the soil sample. Return any worms you find to the soil outside. Then strain the sample into a bowl through the large sieve. Make sure you wash your hands after you have touched the soil.

2 Now pour the soil into the fine sieve and balance it above the jar, as shown above. Position the jar beneath the lamp and wait. After a while, you will see some tiny minibeasts appear in the bottom of the jar.

3 Leave the jar for a few hours, then tip the contents onto the paper towels. Examine the minibeasts closely with a magnifying glass. Use a reference book to identify them, then return them to the soil outside.

WHAT'S HAPPENING

● Tiny creatures in soil prefer cool, damp conditions beneath the ground. The heat from the lamp warms the soil, and the minibeasts try to escape from the heat into the jar below. These small creatures are vital to the soil. They help maintain its goodness by breaking down dead matter and adding nutrients.

KEEPING SOIL HEALTHY

● Each crop adds or removes different nutrients from the soil. For example, corn takes nitrogen out of the soil, while crops called legumes—peas or beans—put nitrogen back into the soil. To keep the soil healthy, many farmers change the crops grown in a field from one year to the next. This is called crop rotation.

Field 1:
1st year: Corn
2nd year: Peas
3rd year: Wheat
4th year: Potatoes

Field 2:
1st year: Peas
2nd year: Wheat
3rd year: Potatoes
4th year: Corn

Field 4:
1st year: Potatoes, 2nd year: Corn
3rd year: Peas, 4th year: Wheat

Field 3:
1st year: Wheat, 2nd year: Potatoes
3rd year: Corn, 4th year: Peas

● Some farmers use insects to help keep the soil healthy. Ladybugs eat aphids, which eat crops. Relationships like this exist within every natural food web. Planting onions between crops can also deter pests without having to use chemical pesticides. Many people prefer to eat food that has been grown this way, called organic food.

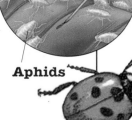
Aphids

Ladybug

LAND USE

Farming has greatly changed the way land is used. Every farm was once natural countryside. Most farming 100 years ago was done on small farms. Today's arable farms often cover huge areas with a single crop, called a monoculture. This is known as intensive farming. Intensive farming can produce more crops than a small farm can, and the crops or products can be sold more cheaply. Machinery and methods have improved so much that far fewer people need to work on the land. But monocultures have changed the environment, too. Wild animals and plants that adapted to small farms, living in meadows and windbreaks, can't find enough food in monocultures.

Wheat

Fruit trees

Poultry

Soybeans

Cattle

Fruit trees

Corn

Some farmers leave uncultivated areas on the edges of fields for wildlife.

WHAT GROWS WHERE?

Make a map to show how land is used for different kinds of farming. You can include small farms and monocultures. You will need paper and some colored pencils.

1 Look at the different kinds of farm shown earlier in this chapter. If there are farms near your home, think about what kinds of farm they are. What crops are growing? Are there any monocultures? Is there any livestock?

2 Choose which farms you want to show on your map. Draw an outline of fields onto the paper.

3 Color your map and design a key. Use different colors to show the type of farming that is being done in each field. Draw symbols for each of the landmarks or buildings on your map.

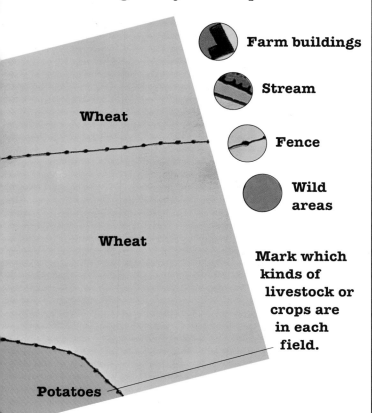

- **Farm buildings**
- **Stream**
- **Fence**
- **Wild areas**

Mark which kinds of livestock or crops are in each field.

Wheat

Wheat

Potatoes

HELPFUL HINTS

● Look at a large-scale map to see if there is any farmland near your house or town. If there is, ask an adult to visit the area with you to look at the kind of farming that is done there.

HABITAT DESTRUCTION

● As natural countryside is plowed up, the wildflowers that grow there are gradually disappearing. The insects that feed on the flowers are going too, which means that birds that feed on the insects are becoming rare. Many songbird species that used to be common on farmland are now endangered.

● Trees and windbreaks help keep the soil in place. Many have been ripped out to make larger fields and, over the years, wind and rain have eroded (worn away) the soil. This has created dustbowls in some areas, where no plants can grow.

● Land around or on farms is often used for recreation. People using the countryside need to follow certain rules to protect the area for farming, wildlife, and for other people to use.

Never leave litter. It can be dangerous for animals.

Keep dogs on a leash so that they do not chase livestock.

TROPICAL FARMING

Many developing countries have tropical climates. In tropical regions, there is a wet season and a dry season, but it is hot all year round. In some places, it is possible to have two harvests in one year. Crops that grow well in tropical climates include coffee, tea, and rice. In the wet season, rainfall is heavy and frequent. On hills, rainwater flows fast down slopes and washes the soil away. This is called soil erosion. Some farmers have learned how to farm slopes by building terraces, like a series of steps.

ON THE TERRACES

To construct your own terraced slope, you will need a deep cardboard box, about 20 inches long and 12 inches wide, a pencil, a craft knife, a trash bag, a plant trough, soil, small stones, and a pitcher of water.

1 Ask an adult to help you cut the cardboard box with the craft knife, so that the sides slope, as shown here. Cut a V-shape in the front. Line the inside of the box with the trash bag.

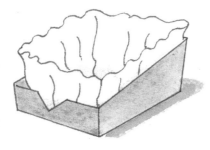

2 Cover the bottom of the lined box with soil. Pile up the soil, so that it is much higher at the back of the box. Position the trough in front, as shown here. Pour water down the slope and watch how easily the soil washes away.

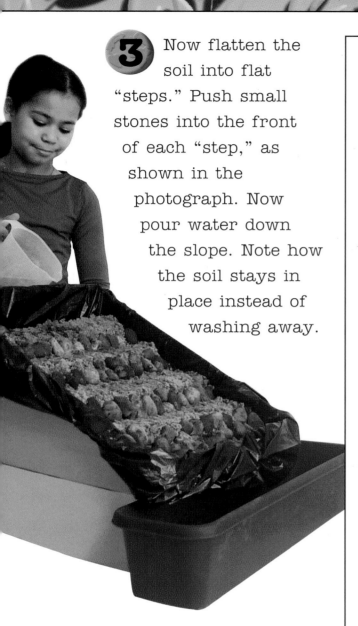

3 Now flatten the soil into flat "steps." Push small stones into the front of each "step," as shown in the photograph. Now pour water down the slope. Note how the soil stays in place instead of washing away.

WHAT'S HAPPENING

● The steps keep the water from flowing too quickly, taking the soil with it. On real terraces, each step is held back by a wall or by plants with strong roots. Ancient Romans planted grapevines and olive trees on terraces. Today, in many parts of Asia, rice is grown on terraced hillsides.

SOIL DEPTH

Humus layer

Temperate   Tropical

● In temperate regions, there is usually a deep layer of humus, which contains all the nutrients in the soil. In tropical regions, the nutrients are quickly taken up by plants, which grow well in the hot, moist conditions. Once the nutrients are used up, the humus layer is thin and the soil is no longer any good for growing crops.

SLASH-AND-BURN

Cassava

● Farmers in tropical areas burn trees and bushes to clear ground for planting crops such as cassava. This is called slash-and-burn, or shifting agriculture, because the farmer has to keep on clearing new land. The ashes from the burned wood are full of nutrients, but new crops use up the nutrients quickly. Soon the soil becomes infertile. The farmer then has to start again and burn another area of forest.

NOT ENOUGH FOOD

Although world food production has increased rapidly in the last 50 years, the population has increased even faster. Millions do not have enough to eat and live close to starvation. Millions more are not able to include some important kinds of food in their diet. One big reason for the lack of food is that farmers wear out the soil as they try to produce more and more food from the same land. Natural disasters such as droughts and floods also destroy crops. Many farmers in developing countries do not have the money to buy machinery and tools to improve their farming conditions.

Salt crust

SALTY SOIL

In some areas, the soil can become too salty to grow crops. You can show how this happens in a simple experiment. You will need a tray, soil, salt, and water.

1 Cover the bottom of the tray with about $1/2$ in of salt. Cover the salt with a layer of soil about 2 in deep. Press down firmly.

2 Pour water over the soil and leave the tray in a warm place. Allow the soil to become dry, then water again. Repeat this a few times.

3 Salt crystals will begin to appear on the top of the soil. After about two weeks, a hard crust of salt will form.

WHAT'S HAPPENING

● When there is too much water, the ground becomes waterlogged. In hot sun, surface water evaporates (dries off) quickly and ground water, which contains salts dissolved from rocks, comes up to the surface. This water also evaporates, and the salt left behind forms salt pans. In the Indus valley in Pakistan (left), floods are frequent, and the soil becomes too salty for crops to grow. Each year, there are 100,000 fewer acres to farm.

SUBSISTENCE FARMING

● Farmers who can only grow enough food for their own families are called subsistence farmers. There is a lot of subsistence farming in developing countries. All the planting and harvesting is done by hand.

In good years, subsistence farmers may grow enough to sell a few crops at local markets. In drought years, when the rains fail, crops wither, and aid agencies must provide food to prevent the farmers and their families from starving.

Hot, dry winds

Dried-up river

Wilted crops

DROUGHT

● A drought happens when the yearly rains in an area are not heavy enough. Crops and grass for cattle shrivel in the heat. Rivers dry up, and people must walk miles to find water. To help areas that suffer drought frequently, scientists are developing fast-growing seeds that survive on low rainfall.

GLOBAL MARKET

Supermarket shelves hold food crops and products from all over the world. Many are grown in plantations, which are vast monocultures with rows of bushes or trees. Pesticides are used so that as many crops as possible can be produced. In tropical regions, huge plantations of tea (below), sugar cane, pineapples, and coffee are common. In temperate regions, fruit is often grown on plantations. Plantations employ many people to pick and pack the crops.

WHERE DOES IT COME FROM?

Make a map showing where crop products come from. You will need food labels, a map, pencils, cardboard, colored pencils, yarn, pushpins, scissors, and glue.

Long-grain rice

Cocoa powder

Lemon juice

Coffee

Sugar

Mango chutney

1 Collect labels from products that come from different countries. Coffee, for example, is grown in Colombia and Kenya. Write down the names of the foods and the names of the countries they come from.

2 Copy a large map of the world. Glue your map onto cardboard, leaving a wide border.

3 Draw and cut out symbols for the food crops you have chosen. Glue the symbols in the correct places on the map. Design and color a key, as shown here.

KEY

Apples Tea

Sugar Rice

Cacao Coffee

Lemons Mangoes

4 Glue your product labels onto the border. Link each one to the correct food crop on the map using lengths of colored yarn and pushpins.

Tea

CASH CROPS

● Crops grown on plantations in tropical countries and sold all over the world are called cash crops. They are grown especially for export, which means to be sold in other countries. Many countries depend on the money from their cash crops. They suffer greatly if world prices for their crops go down, but gain money to improve farming methods if prices are high.

PLANTATION WORKERS

● Workers employed to cultivate cash crops are often poorly paid, but many prefer the work to subsistence farming. In some countries, a "Fair trade" logo appears on products that come from plantations that pay a decent wage to their workers.

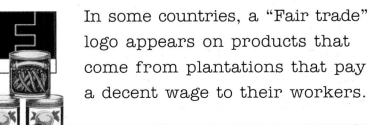

FOOD ON THE MOVE

The banana is a perishable fruit, which means it can rot quickly and lose its value. The banana plant is a huge herb that is so big it is often mistaken for a tree. Huge areas of tropical forest have been cut down so that bananas can be planted as cash crops. Before bananas reach stores, they have a long journey. Look at banana labels to see the many countries in which they are grown. The first bananas grew wild in India. Banana plants were then taken across the world to Central America, where there are now many banana plantations.

1. A stem of bananas can hold 200 bananas, arranged in "hands." Each banana is called a "finger." Workers use a sharp machete, or knife, to cut each stem of green, unripe bananas from the banana plant.

GOING BANANAS

Do an experiment to see how bananas help each other to ripen. You need two unripe bananas, a ripe banana, and two plastic bags.

1 Place one unripe banana in a plastic bag beside the ripe banana. Put the other unripe banana in the second bag.

2 After a few days, compare the bananas. The banana in the bag next to the ripe banana will have ripened faster than the banana in the bag by itself.

WHAT'S HAPPENING

● Bananas naturally produce a gas called ethylene, which makes other bananas ripen. So a ripe banana will make a green banana ripe if they are placed side by side. Just before green bananas reach supermarkets, ethylene gas is used to ripen them quickly.

2. The bananas are loaded into rail trucks, or hung on cables, to be transported for packing. They are washed, cut from their stems, and packed in cartons, then taken to be loaded onto ships.

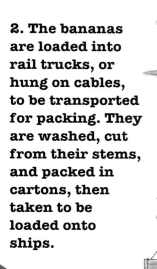

3. Large refrigerated ships carry bananas all over the world. The bananas must still be green when they arrive.

4. Refrigerated trucks meet the ship and swiftly transport the green bananas to supermarket depots.

5. In the supermarket, you can buy fresh bananas all year round.

IMPORTED FOOD

● A long time ago, fruit and vegetables from temperate regions were only on sale after harvest time. Now, shoppers can buy fresh carrots or apples at any time of year. Perishable foods from all over the world are on sale in supermarkets because they can be transported long distances at great speed. Look closely at the labels on fresh fruit and vegetables. Make a note of where they come from, as shown here.

Celery from California

Zucchini from Texas

Chili peppers from Mexico

Grapefruit from Florida

Pears from Oregon

Raspberries from Canada

Apples from South Africa

Cabbage from New York

Mushrooms from Pennsylvania

Asparagus from Michigan

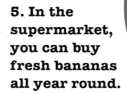
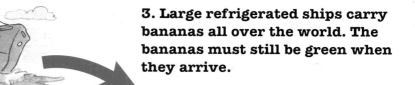

HEALTHY EATING

Food provides us with energy. Most people in developed countries are able to gain enough energy to live healthily by eating a balanced diet, which means eating a variety of foods. In developing countries, it is often more difficult to eat a balanced diet, because farmers are not able to produce enough food for everyone. Farmers and scientists are always trying to develop new farming methods and improve seeds so that more food can be grown, especially in poor soil and poor growing conditions.

A balanced diet includes many kinds of food.

The diet in a developing country may include food from only one or two food groups.

FOOD VALUES

● The body needs four main groups of nutrients to stay healthy, as well as minerals and water. The four groups are carbohydrates, proteins, vitamins, and fats.

Carbohydrates are energy-giving starches in foods such as bread and potatoes; and sugars in foods such as cookies.

Proteins, in meat, eggs, and fish, help growth and repair of the body.

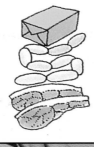

Vitamins are needed to maintain good health. Fruit and vegetables are especially high in certain vitamins.

Fats, in butter and meat, also give the body energy.

WEEKLY FOOD INTAKE

Keep a record of the food you eat every day for a week to find out how balanced your diet is. You will need a notebook, a ruler, and a pencil.

1 Use the ruler to draw five columns in your food intake chart. Write headings for the day and time in the first column, then the four food groups: carbohydrates, proteins, vitamins, and fats, in the other columns.

2 Every time you have a
meal, make a note of
what you eat. Write each piece
of food in the correct column
in your chart. Remember to
include any snacks, such as
chips or fruit, that you eat
between mealtimes.

Weekly food intake

Day/time	Carbos	Proteins	Vitamins	Fats
Monday 7 A.M.	Toast	Eggs	Orange juice	Butter
10.45 A.M.	Chips			
12.30 P.M.	Rice	Chicken	Salad Apple	
4 P.M.	Bread			Peanut butter

3 Check your chart each
day. For a balanced diet,
you should have entries in each
column. The more energy you
use, the more carbohydrates
and fats you need to eat.

IMPROVING FARMING

● To improve and vary
crops, scientists cross
one successful crop
plant with another to produce a new
plant, called a hybrid, that has the best
qualities of both plants.

● Over the last 100 years, wider use
of machinery and intensive research
into seeds, pest control, and soil have
greatly improved food production.
But farmers with no money and poor
growing conditions still struggle.
Scientists continue to develop drought-
resistant and disease-resistant seeds
to help reduce famine in developing
countries.

● Genetically modified (GM) crops
are now being developed and tested.
They may reduce the need for
pesticides and some already give
high crop yields (production).

● Hydroponics is a method of
growing crops without soil. It is
especially useful for testing what
conditions plants need to grow
best. The plant roots are
immersed in a mixture
of water, nutrients,
and sand or gravel.

Nutrient solution

GLOSSARY

acid rain
Rainfall that damages forests because it contains too much acid, caused by air pollution.

altitude
Height above sea level.

arable farming
Crop farming.

atlas
A book of maps.

attrition
The wearing down of pieces of rock carried by wind, water, or ice.

Beaufort scale
A scale from 0 to 12 classifying wind strength.

biome
A large ecosystem, usually named after the type of vegetation that grows there.

camouflage
The use of color or pattern that enables an animal or plant to merge with its surroundings.

carnivore
A meat eater.

cash crops
Crops that are grown especially to be sold in other countries.

climate
The average weather an area has over the year.

compass
An instrument showing the direction of magnetic north.

condensation
The change that occurs when water vapor (a gas) becomes water (a liquid) as a result of cooling.

consumer
An animal or plant that eats other living things.

crystals
Solids with particles arranged in a regular order, forming flat sides or faces.

decomposer
An organism that breaks down dead plant and animal matter, releasing minerals into the soil.

deforestation
The clearing of forest.

deposition
The laying down of eroded material carried by wind, water, or ice.

developed countries
Countries with lots of industries where most people have a high standard of living.

developing countries
Countries with few industries where many people live in poverty.

ecology
The study of ecosystems.

ecosystem
One community in one habitat and its nonliving environment.

environment
The surroundings of a habitat.

equator
An imaginary line around the center of the world. The zero degree (0°) line of latitude.

erosion
The wearing down of the land by natural forces such as waves, wind, and rain.

evaporation
When heat causes water to become water vapor (a gas). The opposite of condensation.

food web
The way in which living things in a habitat rely on each other for food.

fossil fuels
Fuels like coal, oil, and natural gas, formed from remains of living things.

fossil
Evidence of ancient life that is found in sedimentary rocks.

generation
The period of about 20 years that separates parents and children.

geothermal energy
Natural heat from inside the Earth; a renewable source of energy.

geysers
Hot springs that throw up columns of heated water at regular intervals.

global warming
A rise in world temperatures as too much heat is trapped in Earth's atmosphere due to high levels of carbon dioxide caused by burning fossil fuels.

habitat
The natural home of a plant or animal.

hemisphere
Half of the planet Earth. Summer in the northern hemisphere (north of the equator) is winter in the southern hemisphere (south of the equator).

herbivore
A plant eater.

hydroelectric power
Electrical energy that is obtained from generators operated by water turbines.

igneous rocks
New rocks formed either from magma inside the Earth or from lava that has cooled on the surface.

intensive farming
A modern farming practice that uses machinery on large farms to produce large crops cheaply.

irrigation
Any system designed to carry water to the land so that crops will grow.

large-scale maps
Maps that show lots of detail but only small areas of land.

latitude
Distance in degrees north or south of the equator. Lines of latitude are parallel to the equator.

lichen
An organism composed of two living things, algae and fungi.

livestock
Animals that are farmed.

lodestone
A type of rock with magnetic properties that was used as a compass by sailors long ago.

longitude
Distance in degrees east or west of the prime meridian, which is zero degrees (0°) longitude.

magma
Hot, molten (liquid) rock formed deep inside Earth. Called lava when it erupts on the surface.

meander
A bend in a river.

metamorphic rocks
Igneous or sedimentary rocks that have been changed through great heat and pressure inside the Earth.

metropolitan area
Towns and cities joined into one big urban area.

minerals
Substances that make up rocks. In most minerals, particles are arranged in a regular order, forming crystals.

mixed farming
Farming that combines rearing livestock with growing crops.

monoculture
An area in which only one main crop is grown.

oasis
A source of water in hot desert areas, where the water table reaches the surface.

organic farming
Producing crops without using chemical pesticides or fertilizers.

oxbow lake
A lake left where a river cuts through the narrow neck of a meander.

permeable rock
Rock, like limestone, which allows water to soak through cracks and joints.

photosynthesis
The process that plants use to make food, using sunlight and chlorophyll (the green color in leaves).

plantation
A monoculture farm, especially in tropical countries, where cash crops are grown on a large scale.

population density
The average number of people living in each square kilometer or other unit of area.

porous rock
Rock, like sandstone, which allows water to soak through pores or air holes.

predator
An animal that hunts and eats other animals.

prey
An animal hunted and eaten by a predator.

prime meridian
An imaginary line that circles the Earth, north to south, at 0° longitude.

producer
A green plant that makes food through photosynthesis.

refugee
A person seeking shelter from danger by moving to another country.

Richter scale
A scale to measure the strength of earthquakes.

rural
Located in the country.

scale
Representation of size on a map.

sediment
Matter carried by water or wind and deposited on land.

sedimentary rocks
Rocks formed from sediments.

settlement
A place where people live.

small-scale maps
Maps that show little detail but large areas of land.

stalactite
A growth of calcium carbonate that hangs from the roof of a cave in limestone rock.

stalagmite
A column of calcium carbonate that grows upward from the floor of an underground cave in limestone rock.

staple diet
The most common food eaten by people in a region or country.

strata
Layers of rock.

subsistence farming
Small-scale farming, where farmers only grow enough to feed one family.

sustainable farming
Looking after soil and the environment so that the same land can be farmed year after year.

symbiosis
A partnership that benefits two different species.

tectonic plates
Large blocks of Earth's crust that float on the liquid magma beneath.

temperate regions
The parts of the world where temperatures are moderate, and where there is often a marked difference between the seasons.

tributary
Small stream or river that joins a main river.

tropical regions
The parts of the world, near the equator, where the climate is hot all year round. Tropical regions have a wet season and a dry season.

urban
Located in a town or city.

vegetation
Plant life, especially of a particular region.

water table
The level of ground water below which the rock is completely saturated.

INDEX

Children's Department
Marlborough Public Library
35 W. Main St.
Marlborough, MA 01752

PICTURE CREDITS

Abbreviations: t-top, m-middle, b-bottom, r-right, l-left, c-center.

All photographs supplied by Select Pictures, except for: 5tr, 40m, 75mr, 86ml, 93br, 128 all—Digital Stock. 7br, 75bl—NASA. 37tl—Mark Newman/FLPA. 49mr—Bill Broadhurst/FLPA. 51tr, 53tl—Silvestris Fotoservice/FLPA. 52tl, 116c—Derek Hall/FLPA. 58ml—Gary Braasch/CORBIS. 60tr, 64m, 102ml, 137br—Corbis Royalty Free. 62mr—Roger Wood/CORBIS. 66ml—Pat J. Grooves; Ecoscene/CORBIS. 69br—Yann Arthus-Bertrand/CORBIS. 70mr—Michael Busselle/CORBIS. 73ml—Roger Ressmeyer/CORBIS. 75bm—Annie Griffiths Belt/CORBIS. 79bl, 103mr, 136mr, 139t—Stockbyte. 91bl—Rolf Bender/FLPA. 94ml—Jurgen & Christine Sohns/FLPA. 96c—G T Andrewartha/FLPA. 98ml—Ian Rose/FLPA. 101t, 116ml, 116mr, 116blr—David Hosking/FLPA. 117br—Terry Whittaker/FLPA. 122c—Philip Gould/CORBIS. 134mr, 142c—John Deere. 147tl—Galen Rowell/CORBIS. 148ml—Chris Mattison/FLPA.